THE CONSTITUTIONAL LAW OF THE EUROPEAN UNION
Teacher's Manual

Second Edition

James D. Dinnage
Solicitor (England)
Attorney at Law (New York)
Special Legal Consultant (District of Columbia)

John F. Murphy
Professor of International Law and Business
Villanova University School of Law

> **NOTE TO USERS**
> To ensure that you are using the latest materials available in this area, please be sure to periodically check the LexisNexis Law School web site for downloadable updates and supplements at www.lexisnexis.com/lawschool.

Editorial Offices
744 Broad Street, Newark, NJ 07102 (973) 820-2000
201 Mission St., San Francisco, CA 94105-1831 (415) 908-3200
www.lexisnexis.com

MATTHEW◆BENDER

(2008–Pub.3523)

THE CONSTITUTIONAL LAW OF THE EUROPEAN UNION
Teacher's Manual

PREFACE TO THE INSTRUCTORS' MANUAL

The purpose of the manual is simply to assist the instructor at the first level of dialogue with students by providing basic answers to the questions in the NOTES AND QUESTIONS of the Casebook. In many cases the questions should invite further discussion and speculation. There is often no complete and final answer.

The order of materials in the Casebook has, overall, been arranged specifically to enable a logical progression through the subject from the standpoint of how a U.S. constitutional lawyer might approach the subject. It will be noticed however that cases and subject matter often recur in different contexts. This is deliberate. EU law is not an easy subject for U.S. students and the opportunity to illustrate a difficult concept several times from different angles during the course can be helpful.

The book itself contains material that could permit teaching a course over an entire academic year, but it will probably often be used only for a one semester two or three credit course. Given the complexity of the factual situations in many of the cases, our experience has been that, at least in a one semester course, it is advisable to choose a few cases from each chapter for detailed discussion and analysis rather than to try to cover the entirety of the material.

TABLE OF CONTENTS

Part I
THE FOUNDATIONS OF THE EUROPEAN UNION

Chapter 1

ORIENTATION

§ 1.01 OVERVIEW

It may be helpful to begin the course with some introductory remarks such as the following:

1. EU law can seem complex and abstract. Many of the cases relate to areas of national law that will be unfamiliar. These two features make it important to spend time bringing out the facts of the cases. This helps significantly in conveying a true impression of how EU law operates.

2. The term "EU constitutional law" is used in a variety of ways by authors. Compare the content of the Lenaerts and Douglas-Scott works referenced in the text. In this book, the term is used in the way that would be familiar to U.S. law students. This does not mean that EU law is actually structured this way. However, viewing it through a U.S. "lens" helps to put it into a comprehensible framework.

3. This is not a comparative law course but U.S. parallels have been included to help set EU issues in a familiar context.

4. The nature of the case reports — particularly Article 234 references — highlights differences from typical U.S. judgments.

5. Some of the materials assume a basic knowledge of law that might in fact be absent — e.g. public international law, antitrust, administrative law, so it may be necessary to explain some basic concepts from time to time.

6. Note the complexity of the Treaties — these are and have always been a work in progress. Legal issues have often perplexed lawyers and then been erased by new Treaty or Regulation language (e.g. comfort letter issues under Regulation 17; standing of the Parliament under article 230. . . .).

7. The Treaty of Lisbon is covered in the last chapter in anticipation of its entry into force at the end of 2008. References to specific changes occur throughout the book.

8. Explain the article numbering changes. The book uses [ ] to indicate present numbering where old numbering appears in original text, except where the text itself indicates the new numbering as well. All notes and questions use the current numbering.

9. Mention the EU website in particular as an invaluable source of information on almost everything connected with the EU — mention the EU law blog.

10. Law articles — there is a vast collection in all languages. Every ECR case on the EU Eurlex site has its own bibliography. We have referenced articles from time to time where they are particularly helpful to understanding but studying the cases themselves is the best way to gain a grasp of the subject.

11. Urge students to follow developments in the news — this is a living and dynamic subject.

12. Explain that (except in this Chapter) the terms "EU" and "EU Law" are used generically in the Chapter introductions and the Notes and Questions to describe both the European Union as established by the TEU *and* the European Community (which disappears at the end of 2008 and is succeeded by the EU, with references to "Community" being replaced by "Union"). This usage may be technically incorrect for the past, but it simplifies presentation.

A brief verbal introduction of the materials in Chapter 1 may be desirable.

§ 1.02 A CHRONOLOGY OF SIGNIFICANT EVENTS IN EUROPEAN UNIFICATION

- The state of Europe in 1945 and the role of the United States in revitalizing it and avoiding a Communist takeover through the Bretton Woods agreement, the foundation of the German Federal Republic and the Marshall Aid Plan.
- The Franco-German reconciliation starting with the May 9 1950 Schumann declaration regarding the proposed Coal and Steel Community.
- The background to the failed EPC and EDC initiatives — external threats such as Korea/Russian nuclear bomb, Communist takeover in Czechoslovakia etc.
- The Messina conference and the Rome Treaties including importance of Euratom at the time — failure of Britain to endorse.
- The success of the transition period.
- Formation of EFTA.
- DeGaulle intransigeance vs. the UK.
- The politique de la chaise vide — mid-60s — symptomatic of a pull back by Member States from the original EEC as originally conceived.
- The next step — Werner Plan and failure due to the collapse of Bretton Woods/currency instability leading to divergence of economies (inflation — weaker currencies). Failure of the "snake in the tunnel."
- The accession of the UK, Ireland and Denmark in 1973.
- The oil shocks of 1973 and 1979 and the negative effects on integration.
- The re-launch of the plan for EMU through the creation of the basket of currencies central rate in 1979.
- The first direct elections to the European Parliament 1979.
- Accession of Greece, Spain and Portugal.
- The SEA in 1987 and goal of a true internal market by 1992 have a galvanizing effect. Full blooded support of the UK — SEA greatly extends majority voting in the Council and introduces a form of "two chamber" legislative process (co-decision).
- 1989 — Collapse of Berlin Wall and re-unification of Germany — a replay of French concerns regarding strength of Germany drives move to enhance political unification.
- 1992 — Maastricht — the creation the EU as a partnership of sovereign states for political union, plan for monetary union. After the reinforcements of the "Community" competences and institutions in the SEA, TEU is an attempt to limit future development of the Community and move to intergovernmental co-operation as "ever closer union" proceeds.
- Accession of former neutrals — Finland, Austria and Sweden.
- Successful launch of the euro in 1999 for interbank transfers, followed by conversion of currencies in 2002.
- Treaty of Amsterdam in force in 1999 — brings immigration/visa policy into the structure of the EC Treaty.
- Treaty of Nice in force 2002 — largely failed attempt to reform voting procedures in anticipation of further enlargement. Laeken declaration and mandate for an IGC to draft a Constitution for Europe.
- 2004 — accession of 10 new states including former Communist countries — Latvia, Estonia, Lithuania, Poland, Czech Republic, Slovakia, Hungary, Slovenia, Cyprus, Malta.
- Constitution Treaty signed in 2004.

- France and Netherlands referenda defeat ratification of Constitution Treaty although 18 states ratify by 2005.
- Bulgaria and Romania accede. Membership now at 27 States.
- June 2007 agreement on "Reform Treaty" to replace failed Constitution Treaty — contains much the same provisions — designed to avoid need for referenda, with many optouts and variances (the "Europe of footnotes").
- Charter of Fundamental Rights approved by European Parliament on December 12, 2007.
- Reform Treaty renamed Treaty of Lisbon, signed December 13, 2007.

§ 1.03 THE TREATIES FORMING THE CONSTITUTIONAL BASE OF THE EUROPEAN UNION

- ECSC has now disappeared (functions abandoned or absorbed within EC Treaty scope).
- EAEC Treaty continues and the term "Community" is still used for that entity.
- Treaty of Lisbon is an amending treaty.
- EC Treaty will become Treaty on the Functioning of the European Union per the Treaty of Lisbon.
- The TEU will continue in modified form.

§ 1.04 GLOSSARY

The following particular items may benefit from a verbal explanation:

- The process of creating a common market (refer to relevant Treaty provisions)
- Outline of Institutions (refer to relevant Treaty provisions). Highlight dual role of Council in EU/EC and the role of the European Council.
- Legislation processes include Qualified Majority Voting. Institutional balance depends on the pivotal role of the Commission as initiator of legislation within EC Treaty spheres.
- Essential differences between EC and EU Treaties — legislation/role of the Court/European Council/types of legislation.

§ 1.05 CASE REPORTS

Principal sources — ECR/CELEX-LEXIS/CMLR

Citation is not uniform in the literature — e.g. brackets around dates of ECR cases. The Court has changed its usage over the years.

§ 1.06 GENERAL REFERENCE WORKS

EU publications

See the EU homepage — www.europa.eu

Textbooks/Casebooks

Of the general textbooks mentioned, Craig and De Burca is the most up to date and provides a very thorough analysis of almost all topics covered in this casebook.

Useful websites

www.eur-lex.europa.eu/en/index_cnt.html

EU law blog — http://eulaw.typepad.com/eulawblog/

www.blogs.ft.com/brusselsblog/

Part II
_____
THE EUROPEAN UNION AS AN AUTONOMOUS LEGAL SYSTEM

Chapter 2

THE RELATIONSHIP OF EU LAW WITH THE LAW OF THE MEMBER STATES

§ 2.02 SUPREMACY

COSTA v. ENEL
Case 6/64, [1964] ECR 585

Note 1 The Italian government's argument was that since the Italian court had to apply the Italian law, seeking an interpretation under 234 was irrelevant to the decision of the Italian court. The ECJ's view was that since EU law was superior, Article 234 was properly invoked since the Italian court needed to receive the ECJ's views on the various provisions cited in the reference in order then to determine whether in any respect those provisions would render the Italian law unenforceable. Arguably the ECJ did not actually need to find supremacy here, it could have simply ruled that article 234 is unconditional, so the Italian court had the right to ask, and the ECJ had the right to answer, based purely of the national court's determination that it wanted an interpretation.

Note 2 The ruling is based on the need to grant identical effect to EU laws throughout the EU. This could not happen if their application was subject to varying degrees of review by national courts and the contrary application of national law. The logic here may be a little tendentious — after all it presupposes that identical effect is in fact necessary. However, the court falls back on the unique character of the Treaty to arrive at this conclusion.

Note 3 The ECJ did clearly reject the notion that the last-in-time rule prevailed. It did so because the Treaty is superior to national law, not just in conflict with it. The analogy with the U.S is misleading because that would involve looking at the Treaty through the eyes of the domestic constitution. The ECJ could be said to have viewed the Treaty as the equivalent to a constitution in its own right, overriding national constitutions.

Note 4 Q1 The ultimate result in this case illustrates one of the ways that national law can present obstacles to the reception of Community law as superior (see section 4 of this chapter). The Italian referring court was not permitted under Italian law to question Italian statutes, a role reserved for the Italian Constitutional Court.

Q2 — the ECJ has always insisted that it does not rule on validity, but only gives an interpretation, even if the inevitable consequence is that the national court must disapply the national law. As the *IN.CO.GE* case below will illustrate, the Court has considered it appropriate to indicate what EU law requires where a conflict is found.

AMMINISTRAZIONE DELLE FINANZE DELLO STATO v. SIMMENTHAL SPA
Case 106/77, [1978] ECR 629

Note 1 The ECJ's response is entirely focused on the need to ensure that the applicability of EU law is completely unfettered. How the national courts achieve this is left up to them. They could therefore treat conflicting national law as "struck down", or merely suspended or modified with respect to the case before them. There is clearly the risk of a form of legal chaos. However in practice the national courts have found solutions. The IN.CO.GE case immediately following elaborates on this question.

Note 2 The ECJ's ruling could have that effect but the ECJ would say that the Italian state, in subscribing to the EU Treaty, had impliedly undertaken to modify its constitution to allow for the supremacy of EU law. Thus the national court would not in fact be required to act unconstitutionally.

MINISTERO DELLE FINANZE v. IN.CO.GE.'90 SRL AND OTHERS
Joined Cases C-10/97 TO C-22/97, 1998 ECJ CELEX LEXIS 603, [1998] ECR I-6307

Note 1 The ECJ lays out two basic consequences. First, the conflicting national legislation is not "struck down"; it is simply inapplicable in any case where it affects the application of EU law. Second, the inapplicability of the national law requires that the individuals affected be placed financially in the situation they would have been in had the law not been applied to them.

INTERNATIONALE HANDELSGESELLSCHAFT MBH v. EINFUHR- UND VORRATSSTELLE FÜR GETREIDE UND FUTTERMITTEL
Case 11/70, [1970] ECR 1125

Note 1 The ECJ refused to accept that German constitutional freedoms could prevail over EU law, but indicated that EU law enshrined fundamental rights as part of the general principles of law. This theme is now well developed (see the materials in chapter 16) and the problem has thus been minimized, as long as the German courts accept that the EU rights are equivalent. There could still be issues however in terms of the consequences that would ensue from finding that an EU law is invalid because it breaches EU fundamental rights. One consequence could be a legal vacuum. Legal uncertainty is another concern. Perhaps then there remains a possibility of an impasse at some point.

THE QUEEN v. SECRETARY OF STATE FOR TRANSPORT EX PARTE FACTORAME LIMITED AND OTHERS
Case 213/89, [1990] I ECR 2433

Note 2 Under U.K law, the courts were unable to enjoin the enforcement of an Act of Parliament. It is however possible that a case could be engineered that did not require an injunction but merely a decision not to apply the law. One might conjecture that a scenario could arise where, if a vessel were to proceed to engage in fishing and were then arrested, the owners could have asked the court to disapply the British law relating to quota allocation due to the invalidity of the vessel registration provisions. This would avoid the necessity for a direct enjoinder of its enforcement.

Note 3 The next case, *Van Schijndel*, illustrates the kinds of disparities that can arise in degrees of national protection for EU rights. In *Factortame*, it seems unlikely that forum shopping could have occurred since the rule in question was specifically a U.K one. However, one could envisage situations where a party might choose to start proceedings in a particular Member State based on the availability of a procedure or remedy. If the result were that the Member State in question was required to disapply its own law, then other States would take note if they had similar questionable provisions.

JEROEN VAN SCHIJNDEL AND JOHANNES NICOLAAS CORNELIS VAN VEEN v. STICHTING PENSIOENFONDS VOOR FYSIOTHERAPEUTEN
Joined C-430/93 and C-431/93, 1995 ECJ CELEX LEXIS 225, [1995] ECR I-4705

Note 1 The ECJ accepted the approach outlined by the Dutch court. In a civil matter the court is expected to decide only on the basis of the facts and arguments put before it by the litigants and nothing in EU law required the national authorities to change basic procedural premises on which civil litigation was based. Nonetheless the decision is a little surprising given the rulings in cases such as *Simmenthal, Internationale Handelsgesellschaft* and *Factortame*. In those decisions, the Court did not baulk at requiring the national courts to disregard procedural or constitutional constraints. So what was different in *van Schijndel*? The answer at bottom may be purely pragmatic. The national court would have no arguments or facts in front of it on which to bring to bear its own views. One might conclude then that there is a fundamental difference here from the previous line of cases: a conflict with EU law was not a part of the case before the court. Furthermore one could imagine that for the court to introduce issues relating to competition law where potentially serious consequences could result for the parties would be to introduce a form of jeopardy for the parties that they never contemplated when they went forward with their lawsuit.

Such rationale notwithstanding, there is certainly latitude for the judge to suggest certain lines of argument. More importantly, under common law and in civil codes, the court is obliged to raise the issue of public policy as a ground for refusing to enforce a contract. One must therefore conclude in response to these questions that at least in contract cases, it is likely that the court must raise the question of public policy as the underlying basis for invoking EU law and this gives rise to some doubt then of the ECJ's analysis here.

Note 2 There is certainly a weakness in terms of arriving at a consistent result across all Member States. However it is well known that the US Federal Circuit Courts frequently have differed on constitutional issues as well, so the weakness ought not to be considered as peculiar to the EU system, though clearly it is less capable of maintaining cohesion given that the issues have to be dealt with in national courts with their own appeal structures and differences in procedure and evidence.

§ 2.03   DIRECT EFFECT

[A]   Treaty Provisions

VAN   GEND   EN   LOOS   v.   NEDERLANDSE   ADMINISTRATIE   DER BELASTINGEN
Case 26/62, 1963 ECJ CELEX LEXIS 12, [1963] ECR 1

Note 1 Q1 — This case was decided before *Costa*, obviously. The decision is a necessary corollary to *Costa* because it creates the means by which supremacy is turned from a legal concept into a practical reality, just as, in *Marbury v. Madison*, the express supremacy clause of the US Constitution would have been a political concept only if the Courts had not had the ability to pass judgment on the constitutionality of any federal or State law. The practical reality in this case involves the ability of an individual to invoke EU law in the national courts regardless of the standing of treaties in the domestic legal system.

Q2 — As the note implies, who is bound by a treaty's provisions is dependent on the intent of the treaty provision. It would then follow that the same could apply to EC Treaty provisions and indeed the following cases indicate that this is so.

Note 2 Q1/2 — As Note 1 indicates, the Court has tried to make a clear distinction between direct effect and direct applicability. Direct applicability, as the term is used in article 249 means that the act in question is the law of the land without the need for any process of introduction by national legislation. A directly applicable act is the law of the land for private parties as well as government and thus must be applied in proceedings between individuals as well as between individuals and their government. Direct effect by contrast is a doctrine that recognizes that certain provisions of the Treaty and of directives can be asserted by individuals against their government. This will arise only where the act in question creates an unequivocal obligation for the State. The standstill characteristic is the most obvious form of invocable provision. This distinction means that the primacy of EU law, while an absolute in itself, is necessarily constrained by the absence of any legal avenue for challenge of non-invocable acts. In other words, non-invocable provisions by their nature do not permit the national court to determine whether the national law violates the Treaty (or other EU act) or not. This does not mean however that individuals are without remedy if a Member State breaches a non-invocable provision of the Treaty or a directive — an action may lie for compensation against a Member State for breach of EU law whether the law is invocable or not. This is dealt with in detail in chapter 15.

Q3 — Clearly articles 81 and 82; also (see the *Defrenne* case later) article 141.

Note 3 Q1 — It is interesting to note that the court expressly referred to a new order in *international* law. Thus, it clearly was not holding that the Member States had subordinated themselves to a new higher authority that usurped their status as subjects of international law.

Q2 — The ECJ justified its conclusions based on the wording of the preamble, the creation of obligations for individuals and the role of article 234.

Q3 — Had it ruled against invocability, then the Treaty provisions would be subject to varying degrees of implementation based on national constitutional arrangements regarding the effects of Treaties in domestic law and the objectives of a "common market" would have been largely defeated.

Note 4 Q1 — Given the profound effects produced by the *Van Gend* decision, the opinion of the Advocate General failed to grasp the radical nature of the Treaty. He seems to have viewed it entirely in conventional international law vs. domestic law terms and thereby concluded that differing national constitutional provisions on the incorporation of international law into domestic law were an obstacle to the direct effect of Treaty provisions. The ECJ of course reached the opposite conclusion, namely that direct effect was the only way to overcome the differing national treatments. Certainly either interpretation was capable of giving rise to complexities and uncertainties. They are simply a different set of complexities with one leading to a failed common market, the other leading to significant internal legal disruption but supportive of the goals of the Treaty.

Q2 — The AG's approach of course might at first sight be viewed as merely considering the issue raised as a question of interpretation based on the specific wording of the provisions in question. He does not appear to have held the view that none of the Treaty's provisions had direct effect. He simply could not accept that a provision addressed only to Member States could do so.

Unfortunately he then goes on analyze the Treaty's effects in light of the varying treatment the Treaty would have under the Constitutions of the Member States. This clearly missed the point that was central to the Court's decision, namely that the overall intent of the Treaty was to override national constitutions. His whole analysis around the concerns of uncertainty starts from a premise that was fundamentally rejected by the Court.

JOHANNES HENRICUS MARIA VAN BINSBERGEN v. BESTUUR VAN DE BEDRIJFSVERENIGING VOOR DE METAALNIJVERHEID
Case 33/74, [1974] ECR 1299

Note 1 *Van Binsbergen* addressed a provision that appeared to be conditioned on the adoption of EU legislation ("within the framework . . . "). Originally the Treaty provisions that followed article 49 set out a deadline and this enabled the court to attribute direct effect (invocability) to the core prohibition. This deadline, as a practical matter was not met and indeed the pace and scope of legislation designed to resolve issues regarding cross-border services had been pitifully slow. The deadline has since disappeared from the Treaty but by now the invocability of Article 49 has become part of the "acquis".

DEFRENNE v. SOCIETE ANONYME BELGE DE NAVIGATION AERIENNE SABENA
Case 43/75, [1976] ECR 455

Note 1 The provisions of article 141 may be invoked against other private individuals. This difference arises from the interpretation of the section and serves to underscore the interpretative notion of direct effect or invocability, *i.e.*, it shows that the Court will examine the provision to determine on whom obligations are placed by the Treaty.

Note 2 The Court clearly embraced a sunburst concept to deal with the otherwise potentially ruinous consequences of a retroactive ruling. This could be justified on the basis that the Commission itself had not sought to enforce article 141 and indeed had encouraged Member States to believe that the article did not create individual rights. One could have a lively debate as to whether that was fair to all the people who had been discriminated against prior to this case (including Defrenne herself).

[B] Directives

VAN DUYN v. HOME OFFICE
Case 41/74, 1974 ECJ CELEX LEXIS 124, [1974] ECR 1337

Note 1 (All questions) — Although not articulated in the judgment, the distinction drawn in article 249 may be addressing the question as to who is affected by the *obligations* in that legislation. Regulations *bind everyone* falling within their subject-matter, while directives generally *bind only the Member States*. This does not however answer the question as to who might have *rights* under such legislation. Article 249 does not address that question and thus it was open to the ECJ to arrive at its own conclusion on that point. This point comes clearly into focus when the court is considering the "horizontal" effects of directives, as will be seen specifically in the *Berlusconi* case in chapter 3).

Given the above rationale, one can then conclude that the role of the Member States is not undermined — it is still *their* responsibility alone to implement directives and until they do so individuals cannot be bound by them.

Note 4 The role of the English court would now be to determine whether the Government's order met the test in the Directive — it would need to determine only whether the UK government's reasons for barring Ms Van Duyn were related to her personal conduct. This could however include her association with Scientology, as the Court went on to indicate (for this aspect of the case, see the further extract in Chapter 16). There could still be a difference of interpretation and fact finding procedures of course that might lead to inconsistent applications in various member States, but this seems not very different from how federal law application may differ from one court to another in the U.S..

MARSHALL v. SOUTHAMPTON & SOUTH WEST HAMPSHIRE AREA HEALTH AUTHORITY
Case 152/84, [1986] ECR 723

Note 1 Q1 — as discussed earlier, a directive can be invoked only against a Member State. There is a distinct possibility however that an individual who is discriminated against could sue that state for compensation, even though he or she could not sue the employers. More on this can be found in chapter 15.

Q2 — The artificiality is created by the nature of a directive, and can be overcome by adoption of the appropriate state legislation.

CRIMINAL PROCEEDINGS AGAINST RAFAEL RUIZ BERNALDEZ
C-129/94, 1996 ECJ CELEX LEXIS 205, [1996] ECR I-1829

Note 1 The result of the Court's interpretation is that the exclusion for property damage in the policy was invalid since the law under which it existed was contrary to the directive. Hence, the insurer found itself with a liability that it thought it did not have. The ECJ pointed out that it could recover the payout from the insured, but this seems a flimsy compensation at best.

[C]   Decisions Addressed to Member States

GRAD v. FINANZAMT TRAUNSTEIN
Case 9/70, [1970] ECR 825

Note 1 The precise provision held to be invocable here was only an implied standstill regarding the introduction of taxes not in conformity with the plan to introduce the turnover tax (VAT). This is certainly a step beyond the typical characteristics of direct effect (invocability) but seems logical enough. It could raise factual issues as to what constitutes an "introduction" or "re-introduction" of a measure, but this could be for the national court to determine.

Note 2 (All Questions) — It might initially be apparent from the judgment that the ECJ perceives decisions addressed to Member States to be analogous to directives; thus they are capable of producing direct effects if their provisions meet the standards for directives or treaty provisions. What is interesting about this case however is that it highlights the different role that decisions can play compared with directives. In this instance the decision was a step towards implementation of a common transport policy, *i.e.* the creation of a body of EU law rather than harmonization of national law. Ultimately such a policy requires the adoption of regulations, which would be enforceable *against* private individuals. Would it not then be possible to argue that decisions such as the one at issue here ought to be viewed more like regulations? There is certainly precedent for treating some Regulations as "bundles of decisions" (see chapter 14 and also the wording of article 230). In *Simmenthal S.p.A. v. Commission*, Case 92/78, [1979] ECR 777 (See infra, Chapter 14), the Court was willing to find that executive actions taken in the context of implementation of a regulation should be treated as "regulations" for the purpose of article 241.

§ 2.04   THE DUTY OF SINCERE COOPERATION

VON COLSON & KAMANN v. LAND NORDRHEIN-WESTFALEN
Case 14/83, [1984] ECR 1891

Note 1 If the notion of compliant interpretation is stretched to the limit, it means that national legislation, which does create rights against private individuals, should be interpreted as though it did indeed follow the directive. Thus the directive is not invoked as such, but indirectly obviously the result is the same as if it had been.

Note 4 It might be conjectured that the ECJ will look at the intent of the directive and conclude that, where it indeed addresses relationships between individuals, the compliant interpretation doctrine should be rigorously applied to an extent where even a manifest contradiction could be overlooked in favor of implementing the directive. The principle that directives only bind Member States starts to look very tenuous at that point. Nonetheless, the ECJ is unlikely to change its stance regarding the legal effect of directives as a matter of principle, particularly where the possibility of compensation against the state for the wrongdoing of individuals could achieve the same practical result. In consequence, Member State courts might be expected to develop legal presumptions that an inadequate implementing law must be deemed to incorporate the right built into the underlying directive. The Court has made it clear however that under no circumstances can directives create criminal offenses or penalties absent national law to that effect — see for example the *Berlusconi* case in Chapter 3.

Note 6 According to the ECJ, each Member State is entitled to defend its own interests in the Council: *Portugal and Spain v. Council* Joined Cases C-63/90 and 67/90, 1992 ECJ CELEX LEXIS 151, [1992] ECR I — 5073:

> "53 The adoption of a legislative measure by the Council cannot constitute either a breach of the obligation imposed on the Member States to guarantee the application and effectiveness of Community law, the defence by each Member State of its interests within the Council manifestly not falling within the scope of that obligation, or a breach of the duty of sincere cooperation attaching to the Council as an institution."

§ 2.05   REACTIONS TO THE DOCTRINE OF SUPREMACY IN THE COURTS OF THE MEMBER STATES

[A]   Acceptance of the New Legal Order

ADMINISTRATION DES DOUANES v. SOCIETE CAFES JACQUES VABRE & J. WEIGEL ET CIE SARL
COUR DE CASSATION (COMBINED CHAMBERS)
[1974] CASS. CH. MIX. 6, [1975] 2 CMLR 336 (MAY 24, 1975)
(France)

Note 1 The court in *Vabre* seems to have been very much in agreement with the Procureur Général in holding that any issue that article 55 of the French Constitution might pose was irrelevant because it was bound to accept the Treaty as creating a new legal order which required precedence over national legislation.

Note 6 No. The ECJ has consistently deferred to existing national procedures and thus recognized that the manner in which EU law issues are considered in relation to domestic law will necessarily vary. This is evident for example in the *Van Schijndel* case. See also the cases on this subject in Chapter 15, *infra*. It would be interesting to speculate on how the ECJ might view the legislative history of legislation which clearly showed a deliberate intent to ignore relevant EU legislation. Perhaps in such circumstances the ECJ might consider that national systems should provide a mechanism to challenge such legislation after enactment even in the absence of a case or controversy.

[B]   Conflicts With Fundamental Rights and Other Constitutional Requirements

INTERNATIONALE HANDELSGESELLSHAFT MBH v. EINFUHR-UND VORRATSSTELLE FÜR GETREIDE UND FUTTERMITTEL (SOLANGE I)
CASE 2 BVL 52/71, 37 BVERFGE 271, [1974] 2 CMLR 540 Federal Constitutional Court (2nd Senate)
(Germany)

Note 1 (All Questions) — The apprehensions of the majority opinion in the 1974 decision were obviously allayed, but it is not clear they were entirely dispelled given the continued absence of an enacted body of fundamental rights. Thus, the potential for a conflict with EU law continues. Moreover, the EU Treaty now contains a reference to the European Convention of Human Rights (article 6 (2)) along with a reference to national rights, as sources of "fundamental rights" which the EU is to respect. The Treaty of Lisbon would incorporate the Charter of Fundamental Rights (first drawn up and proclaimed in the 1970s) into EU Law on a par with the founding Treaties.

The later ruling still does not really amount to an acceptance of supremacy but rather a continued viewpoint that, ultimately, it is for the German courts to apply the German Constitution. Put another way, as long as the discussion continues to focus on whether or not legal developments in the EU meet German requirements, one cannot conclude that the supremacy concept of the ECJ has been endorsed. Note that the Constitution Treaty had contained a clear statement on supremacy, but this has been banished in the Treaty of Lisbon to Declaration No 29 which simply states that it is the opinion of the Council's Legal Service that the case law of the Court confirms that EU law has primacy over national law. The postulate that the ECJ might uphold legislation that the German Courts considered to be contrary to German fundamental rights remains as a potential hazard. It seems from the Solange II case and the bananas litigation that differences in interpretation of similar principles might lead to different results at the German vs. the European level but this might not be enough to trigger the sort of concerns alluded to by the German Court. Furthermore, assuming the Treaty of Lisbon becomes effective, the EU will become a signatory to the ECHR, which should further assist in uniformity of approach or at least provide reassurance that such uniformity is intended.

Note 3 This question invites the class to speculate on the problems that could arise and the possible solutions. In practice one could imagine that the national courts will continue to find ways to sidestep the issue. If not, then there would have to be a constitutional amendment, failing which, Germany could ultimately be found out of compliance and fined (see further chapter 13, *infra*). A crisis of this kind seems highly unlikely because it presupposes that the national courts are willing to take on as a legal issue what is really a political choice. Such a "meltdown" would probably be symptomatic of something much more serious.

Note 5 Q1/2 — the materials in chapters 6, 7 and 16 will clearly demonstrate that the ECJ has found a solution to the balancing implied here. The cases in those chapters will illustrate an approach where, in the case of legislation not directly intended to affect free movement rights, the national courts are entitled to consider whether the national legislation pursues legitimate goals that, as long as they are not in fact disguised attempts to restrict free movement, may justify such legislation. Moreover, the free movement rights are subject to EU fundamental rights as well.

Q3 — Article 295 has been almost totally ignored by EU jurisprudence. It has always been assumed that it was merely a saving provision to ensure that property rights in the narrow sense were not affected. Yet even in that sense the ECJ has essentially ignored it — see chapter 8 *infra* for materials illustrating how intellectual property rights have been redefined to meet the requirements of articles 28 and 30.

Q4 — later cases have indicated that the ECJ is very unwilling to allow the "free movement" provisions such as those on services to override state fundamental rights. It has avoided conflicts either by reading into the various prohibitions a "rule of reason" for situations involving an indirect effect of these provisions (See Chapter 6, *infra*), or (on one reading) by considering that the freedom of movement is itself subject to fundamental rights — see the *Schmidberger* case in Chapter 17. As noted there, if the Charter of Fundamental Rights becomes a part of EU law as intended by the Treaty of Lisbon, a balancing would be necessary between two EU principles. The Charter, like the ECHR however, expressly contemplates the need for balancing of individual rights vs. social and cultural needs.

Q5 — one might conclude that, with some sovereign rights now exercised by the EU, or in common with the EU, this constitutional provision has been bypassed. However, one could also take the position that the Irish have used referendums to ratify membership and major amendments, so that the article has been respected. This issue probably arises in almost every Member State and the general view of the States is that the EU exercises conferred powers. As long as such powers have been conferred in a way authorized by the Constitution, that conferral would be regarded as compliant with it even if the result is that binding legislation emanates from an external body.

Note 6 The question of mandatory referral is considered in Chapter 15, *infra*. In subsection (g) of this section of the chapter, there are cases that demonstrate a readiness on the part of the national courts to take decisions themselves. The Chapter 15 materials look more closely at whether this could be a violation of article 234, but the practical reality is that in many cases, the ECJ has no means of interfering.

[C]   Restrictions on the Transfer of Sovereignty

BRUNNER v. EUROPEAN UNION TREATY
Cases 2 BvR 2134/92 and 2159/92, [1994] 1 CMLR 57 (Federal Constitutional Court, second chamber, October 12, 1993)
(Germany)

Note 1 The court's description of the EU as a means by which the Member States exercise their sovereignty in common is arguably an accurate statement with respect to the *pre-Treaty of Lisbon* arrangement where the EU does not have legal personality. As suggested in Chapter 1, *supra*, the EU can be viewed as having been a sort of "general partnership" where, within its scope, the partners, acting unanimously, determine matters of policy which they then implement individually or delegate to the EU Institutions.

As regards the EC Treaty, one might take issue with the implications of the court's analysis, in light of the *Costa* and *Van Gend* judgments. The ECJ referred to "limitations of sovereign rights" and indeed to a "transfer of sovereign rights" in *Costa*. The logic underlying the ECJ's conclusions (new legal order, direct effects within the Member States, "effectiveness") all point to the creation of an independent "sovereign" body, not one where the authority of its law is dependent on the Constitutions of the member- States. Of course, the judgment only needed to address the propriety of Germany's ratification of the EU Treaty, but the description of the role of the EU within the EC Treaty is troubling. In the next chapter, the Italian Constitution court case of *Merlini* likened the ECSC to a body corporate, thus capable of making its own decisions separate from and not on behalf of its shareholders or members. This is a more attractive analogy although (as will be pointed out) not entirely satisfactory since the EU then has to implement most of its actions through its "shareholders".

BLACKBURN v. ATTORNEY GENERAL
[1971] C.M.L.R. 784, 1 W.L.R. 1037 (1971) (Court of Appeal)
(United Kingdom)

Note 2 The supremacy of Parliament is the only constitutional rule that one could say for certain exists in the United Kingdom. To abandon it would leave a vacuum that the courts would not want to fill, so it is entirely unlikely that they will recognize that it has been compromised in any way. The *Thoburn* case *infra* offers a pragmatic solution that preserves the doctrine while accommodating the ECJ doctrine.

[D]   Hierarchy of Laws/Repeal by Subsequent Enactment

RAOUL GEORGES NICOLO AND ANOTHER
[1990] 1 CMLR 173
Conseil d'Etat
(France)

Note 1 The Commissaire du Gouvernement clearly considered that the supremacy of EU law was not an EU matter but a question of interpretation of Article 55, concluding that it gave precedence to Treaties generally, whether entered into before or after any conflicting legislation. As a practical matter this would provide the French courts with a satisfactory rationale for according supremacy, but it clearly is insufficient to meet the *Costa* standard, since supremacy would be vulnerable to a change in the Constitution.

Note 3 Correct, for the reasons given in note 1.

MCCARTHY'S LTD v. SMITH
COURT OF APPEAL (CIVIL DIVISION)
[1979] 3 AN SR 725 [1979] 3 CMLR 44
(United Kingdom)

THOBURN v. SUNDERLAND CITY COUNCIL; HUNT v. HACKNEY LONDON BOROUGH COUNCIL; HARMAN AND ANOTHER v. CORNWALL COUNTY COUNCIL; COLLINS v. SUTTON LONDON BOROUGH COUNCIL
Queen's Bench Division
[2002] EWHC 195 (Admin), [2003] QB 151
(United Kingdom)

Note 1 Q1/2 — The use of an ordinary statute obviously is more likely to lead to conflicts if it is considered to be the only route by which EU law is effective within a Member State. Any subsequent statute having equal standing that conflicts with an earlier measure could override it. This problem was addressed in *Thoburn*, and in the case of the UK, indicates a dramatic shift in common law doctrine.

Q3 — No, since the ECA merely offers the conduit for the direct application of regulations, it doesn't purport to re-enact them in detail through dedicated legislation.

Note 3 Q1 — The court clearly didn't accept that the ECJ's view of EU supremacy was a part of the English legal system. As with so many of these national cases, the courts continue to feel bound within the constraints of their own constitutions and thus try to find pragmatic solutions that achieve the ECJ's desired result without effecting a legal revolution. Laws LJ clearly enunciated a confirmation of Sankey VC's observation that some statutes simply cannot be repealed and included the ECA in that category, indeed it is the example par excellence.

Q2 — The only way that EU law would cease to be supreme would be where the UK withdrew from the EU by mutual agreement with the other Member States. (Note that in the Treaty of Lisbon an express right of withdrawal is now to become part of the TEU.) In that sense the doctrine of the sovereignty of Parliament is preserved and a confrontation is averted. It should be noted however that the notion that there is a hierarchy of statutes is entirely an invention of the common law over the last 50 years or so, to deal with political realities.

[E]   Procedural Obstacles

FACTORTAME LTD. AND OTHERS, APPELLANTS AND SECRETARY OF STATE FOR TRANSPORT, RESPONDENT
[On appeal from REGINA v. SECRETARY OF STATE FOR TRANSPORT, Ex parte FACTORTAME LTD. AND OTHERS]
[HOUSE OF LORDS] [1990] 2 AC 85
(United Kingdom)

Note 1 The real concern of Lord Bridge here is not the discomfort of issuing an injunction against the Crown as such, notwithstanding the contradiction inherent in such an action — the Crown effectively enjoining itself. Indeed, as the full judgment indicates, there are circumstances where the courts are quite comfortable enjoining a government minister from taking illegal action. The problem identified by Lord Bridge was that the courts were placed in a situation where they could effectively be requiring a Minister to do something that ultimately would turn out to be illegal — ie disapplying an Act of Parliament. One can surely have some sympathy with this concern! Of course, had that turned out to be the case, Parliament could have "pardoned" the Minister. In any event, by declining initially to grant an injunction, the courts were then instrumental in placing the UK government ultimately in the position of having to pay damages for the damage incurred by enforcing the legislation until the ECJ gave its ruling and the English courts proceeded to issue the injunction. Of course, one can easily recognize that the government should have known better than to violate EU law in quite such a flagrant way (though some would argue the point was not actually that clear and if it had been, no reference was really necessary).

[F] Unilateral Determinations on the Scope and Meaning of EU Law

MINISTRE DE L'INTERIEUR v. COHN-BENDIT
Conseil d'Etat (Assemblée), [1978] Recueil Lebon 524, [1979] Receuil Dalloz 155, [1980] 1 CMLR 543, Dec 22, 1978
(France)

Note 1 Q1 — While the Conseil might be right in general terms regarding the legal effects of directives, the statement that they cannot be invoked by individuals is clearly out of line with the ECJ's interpretation. Moreover, the conclusion that a reference to the ECJ was improper is simply wrong. This was a relatively early case of course, but today, one may reasonably assert that, except in the case of wilful abuse perhaps, if any judge decides, however misguidedly, that an interpretation of Community legislation is required, he or she should be free to make the reference.

Q2 — Yes: the question whether a given area of policy falls within the scope of the EU Treaties is clearly a matter of interpretation of the respective Treaty, so it is hard to understand why the minority would assume that the national court was entitled to make that threshold determination unilaterally.

Note 2 It is hard to fault a national court in deciding not to make a reference where the likelihood is that the ECJ would not throw any further light on the subject. Here, (as will be seen in Chapter 15) the ECJ would probably have confined itself to confirming that the directive in question certainly encompassed indirect discrimination and that the national court as fact finder would then have to determine whether discrimination in fact occurred. This was what the Irish court ordered the lower courts to do.

Note 3 The proposition inherent in the Spanish Court's judgment here is that mere procedural requirements cannot rise to the level of an EU issue. There is no support for such a notion in the jurisprudence of the ECJ. That is not to say that the ECJ would necessarily have objected to the rule in question, since it does not appear unreasonable in principle. The question would be whether it was proportionate in terms of the policy reason for its existence. (see further chapter 15, *infra*)

Note 4 Q1 — In general terms such issues would be unlikely to arise because federal law exists as a separate legal system alongside state law, with its own system of enforcement.

Q2 — As noted elsewhere, if state officials refuse to obey federal law, they may be subject to arrest by federal marshals, who also have the power to enforce compliance. No such organization exists in Europe. The primacy and invocability of EU law are left in the hands of state courts, and a wilful failure to comply would go unremedied unless the Commission brings proceedings against the Member State in a separate article 226 action which clearly is not comparable to the direct enforcement of federal law.

Q3 — Both federal and state laws are subject to judicial review against the requirements of the US Constitution. Violation of a constitutional requirement will lead to the invalidity of the law. On the other hand, conflicts between state and federal laws is viewed in light of the doctrine of "preemption" which entails a more pragmatic analysis of the intent and reach of the federal law — this is discussed further in chapter 5.

Q4 — In the EU context, there are certain Treaty articles that might be regarded as constitutional in nature: the articles such as those invoked in *Costa* and *Van Gend* are, as will be seen in Part III, equivalent to the dormant commerce clause principle in the U.S. and therefore any state statute that violates them is *per se* unenforceable. However, this is not really the same legal effect as would occur in the U.S., where the offending state statute is "struck down". One might therefore conclude that EU law should be seen more as a sort of infiltration of state constitutions and legal systems, creating inviolable norms within the legal order of the states, rather than an independent system of law which periodically collides with and then prevails over state legislation. This leads us directly into the first section of chapter 3 which explores to what extent EU law fits this model or can be seen as a separate body of "federal" law.

Chapter 3

THE COMPONENTS OF EU LAW

§ 3.02   THE TREATIES AND OTHER ACTS

[General Note: the cases in this section 3.02 are intended to explore the extent to which the Treaties serve as constitutional documents.]

[A]   Standing as an Autonomous Body of Law

ACCIAIERIE SAN MICHELE SPA (IN LIQUIDATION) v. HIGH AUTHORITY OF THE ECSC
Constitutional Court, [1966] I, 1 Giur. It. 193, [1965] I Foro It. 8, [1967] CMLR 160
(Italy)

Note 2 The Italian Court concluded that while the ECJ was not a regular Court, because its powers and judgments were only incorporated into Italian law by an ordinary law rather than being part of the Constitutional judicial structure of the Italian state. This, one surmises, would have meant that its judgments could not be enforced in Italy since the court was not recognized as a valid judicial tribunal by the Constitution. The Italian court rejected this notion, noting that the ECJ's authority stemmed from the act of ratification by the Italian State of the ECSC Treaty. The ECJ could not be concerned with what internal arrangements might exist for according court judgments the power of binding decisions. Thus, the decision seems to affirm that the Treaty indeed exists as an autonomous body of law. The same logic would seem to extend to the EU, though the ECJ and CFI do not have the power to impose levies or penalties directly on individuals, (other than through the Commission in the case of articles 81 and 82 violations) so the case itself is of historical interest (given that the ECSC Treaty has expired).

HIGH   AUTHORITY   OF   THE   ECSC   v.   CONCORDATO   OFFICINE ELETTROMECCANICHE MERLINI
[1964] CMLR 184
(Italy)

Note 1 The plaintiffs' argument was essentially that the tax in issue here should be accorded preference because it was in effect a tax levied by the Italian state, exercising its sovereignty through the ECSC. In fact the court concluded the opposite — that the ECSC was an autonomous body that exercised its powers through the Member States. Again, this seems to be equally applicable to the EU. However, the analogy seems to falter once one takes into consideration that one arm of the lawmaking process — the Parliament — is now directly elected by the populations of the Member States, thus bypassing the States as "shareholders" or "directors."

MACLAINE WATSON & CO LTD v. DEPARTMENT OF TRADE AND INDUSTRY AND RELATED APPEALS
[1989] 1 CH 72, 253, 286, 309, [1988] 3 ALL ER 257
(C.A. civ. div. April 27, 1988)
(United Kingdom)

Note 1 The English court looked for help from the provisions of the Treaties relating to the privileges and immunities of the EU and found nothing to support a sovereign immunity argument. This could be viewed as a pragmatic approach but does not in any way reflect a concept of a sovereign autonomous body acting independently of the Member States in the way that the Italian court in Merlini did. It does not follow however that on this particular issue, the Italian courts, had they been faced with it, would have come to a different conclusion. Unlike the United States there is no separate system of EU Courts and it is therefore necessary to raise EU issues in state courts — as expressly recognized by article 234. Hence it could scarcely be seen as an affront to the EU's sovereignty if it is sued there. This then means the national courts would not reject a suit on that ground. Nor would they (per *Merlini*) likely accept any argument that the (then European Community) was an emanation of the state (which, if that were the case might protect it from suit). Thus there seems no practical way to deal with sovereign immunity other than in the way that the English court did so.

Note 2 It is likely that the ECJ would focus on Article 10 as well as the other Treaty and Protocol provisions. (See the *Hurd* case in note 4). It would also express a desire for uniform treatment of the issue in the Member States. It might then refer to principles of international law and lay down some baselines for national law on this subject. Since the UK rules generally reflect the trend in international law in refusing immunity to states and organizations engaged in commercial activities, the ECJ would probably have been content to let the UK courts determine whether the UK law complied with the basic principles and the case would not have been decided any differently.

Note 4 The taxation of EU employees by the Member States where they work does not seem to imply any sovereignty issues because this concerns their private income, not therefore affecting the EU. The same is true in the U.S. State and Municipal bonds are treated differently because of the direct effect that taxation would have on their ability to raise funds, and thus would be a drain on their resources, much as the taxation in the *Hurd* case (since although private income was involved, the school would have incurred the additional expense of grossing up the payments, so taxation would have cost the EU more than it would otherwise have).

OPINION 1/91
RE THE DRAFT TREATY ON A EUROPEAN ECONOMIC AREA
1991 ECJ CELEX LEXIS 479, [1991] ECR I-6079

OPINION 1/92
RE THE DRAFT TREATY ON A EUROPEAN ECONOMIC AREA
[1992] ECR 2821

Note 1 Q1 — The ECJ first outlined the essential principle guiding its approach, namely that the EU and the EEA pursue fundamentally different objectives. The EU is a dynamic organization that is constantly moving forward to closer integration, while the EEA is simply a reactive organization. Thus, while the provisions of the two treaties might read identically, there is no guarantee that they will be interpreted the same way going forward. Furthermore, the EEA treaty did not properly recognize the primacy of EU law, but merely provided for national legislature to assure that national laws should not be contrary to its provisions — which would clearly be inappropriate for the Member States, who were also parties to this Treaty, since EU law goes further than that.

Given these two fundamental concerns, the Court proceeded to examine the Draft EEA Treaty to discover whether the homogeneity of the EU system was protected.

It found that a number of the EEA provisions would jeopardize the autonomy of the EU system:

(a) Requirement for the EEA Court to follow Court of Justice decisions did not apply to future judgments;

(b) The power of the EEA Court implicitly to rule on the division of competences between the EU and the Member States

(c) Power of the EEA Court to rule on EEA rules that are incorporated directly into the EU legal system and sit alongside the corresponding EU rules would contravene the requirement in Article 220 that the ECJ would be the sole court responsible for interpreting EU law;

(d) (Given the initial underlying concerns), placing of ECJ judges in the EEA Court would require them to take differing approaches to the same rules, which would place them in an impossible position;

(e) The non-binding nature of judgments given by the ECJ in response from EFTA Courts. Here the Court fundamentally objected to the notion that it could serve as an advisory body, a function it considered at odds with its role as a court of law.

Q2 — It is inconceivable the U.S. Supreme Court would be asked to share powers with third country judges in this way. In that regard, the ECJ's reaction to the original EEA agreement does reflect a very clear and principled approach to the autonomy and sovereignty of the EU.

Q3 — The Court noted that changes had been made with the goal of preserving the autonomy of the EU legal order:

(a) The revised treaty abandoned the proposal for an EEA Court together with the notion that decisions of the combined court would have identical effects in the EEA and the EU.

(b) The Treaty now established a Joint Committee charged with keeping under review the decisions of the EFTA court and the ECJ (art 105). The Joint Committee's decisions however must not affect the case-law of the ECJ. If the Joint Committee could not reconcile conflicting interpretations, there was a further procedure for settling the dispute (art 111). The ECJ was concerned that this might be construed as giving to the Joint Committee the power to give a binding interpretation of EU law, but concluded that, by linking articles 105 (which denied it the power to do so at the earlier stage) and 111, it was intended that the Joint Committee could not make a determination that affected the ECJ's case law.

(c) To the extent that the ECJ was asked to give opinions to the Joint committee, although such rulings were not intended to settle the dispute, they would be binding as to the interpretation given, thus not undermining the role of the ECJ as a court.

[B] Fundamental Rights as an Integral Element of the Constitutional Structure

LISELOTTE HAUER v. LAND RHEINLAND — PFALZ
Case 44/79 [1979] ECR 3727

Note 1. Q1 — Fundamental rights find their way into the EC Treaty via the requirement in Article 220 that the ECJ is obliged to ensure that the law is observed. The Court takes that statement as an invitation to import principles common to the Member States as further defined in the European Convention on Human Rights (now specifically endorsed by the TEU, Article 6). This might be compared with the introduction of the Federal Bill of Rights in the U.S. where the guarantees of basic rights under State laws and constitutions were perhaps not thought to extend to federal actions or at any rate were not sufficiently developed to allow a concept of "principles common to the States."

Q2/3 — It was clearly vital that the ECJ find that fundamental rights are part of EU law because of the danger that the German Courts might otherwise start denying effect to EU laws. The ECJ was able to determine enough commonality in the rules to recognize that in the EU Member States, property rights were subject to a general social interest that could require owners not to use their land for certain purposes. The

Court was influenced by the objectives of the Treaty only in the sense that they were a reflection of the kind of social interest that could override property rights.

[C]   Protocols, Declarations and Agreements Adopted in the EU Framework

COMMISSION v. SPAIN
(VISAS FOR THIRD COUNTRY NATIONALS)
Case C-503/03, 2006 ECJ CELEX LEXIS 171, [2006] ECR I-1097

Note 1 Q1 — The ECJ lays down clearly that the language of this particular protocol must be read subject to the superior rules contained in the Treaty text itself because it expressly says so. But suppose that a protocol is silent on this question? It seems difficult to conceive of a case where the Court would consider any protocol impliedly overrides a Treaty provision but clearly an express override would do so, in fact that is largely the purpose of many protocols — as for example the opt-out provisions (now repealed) regarding the application of the social chapter in the UK.

Q2 — It seems unlikely that there could arise a direct conflict with a preamble statement because these are necessarily outlines and are not intended to create specific obligations. The issue arose during the negotiations for the Treaty of Lisbon where France had insisted on deletion of references to undistorted competition as a goal of the Union (which had been in the Constitution Treaty but not in the EC Treaty). The UK succeeded then in having a protocol added (No 5) that spoke about the Union taking action to enforce competition — it would surely seem that the absence of a preamble goal could not be used to negate 50 years of policy in this area, while the presence of the protocol merely seems to state the obvious. In future years, people may wonder what exactly it is supposed to achieve.

§ 3.03   LEGISLATION AND EXECUTIVE ACTS

[A]   Regulations Contrasted with Decisions

CONFEDERATION NATIONALE DES PRODUCTEURS DE FRUITS ET LEGUMES v. COUNCIL
Joined Cases 16 & 17/62, [1962] ECR 471

ZUCKERFABRIK WATENSTEDT GMBH v. COUNCIL
Case 6/68, [1968] ECR 409

Note 1 (Both Questions) — The ECJ's approach to the question appears at first glance to have undergone a considerable evolution between Confédération and Zuckerfabrik. In the earlier case it focused on the question as to whether the measure was "concerned with designated persons individually." This might then suggest that if a measure could be viewed as addressing a "closed class" of persons, it might qualify as a decision. In *Zuckerfabrik*, the ECJ emphasized instead the *character* of the measure — did it apply to "objectively determined situations and have effects on classes of persons defined in a general and abstract manner." Thus, even if it applied to a closed class, it would still, with these characteristics be considered a regulation. This later formulation was generally helpful because it enabled a clear distinction to be drawn between the definitional exercise and the separate question as to whether, having defined the measure, it would be considered of direct and individual concern for the purposes of Article 230.

Note 2 An individual would still potentially have recourse to an action for damages — see Chapter 14.

Note 3 The ECJ has been constantly vigilant in assuring that the right forms and procedures are used. Any distortions of the kind suggested would not be tolerated.

AHMED ALI YUSUF AND AL BARAKAAT INTERNATIONAL FOUNDATION v. COUNCIL AND COMMISSION
Case T-306/01, 2005 ECJ CELEX LEXIS 422, [2005] ECR II 3533

COMAFRICA SPA AND DOLE FRESH FRUIT EUROPE LTD & CO v. COMMISSION
Case T-139/01, 2005 ECJ CELEX LEXIS 37, [2005] ECR II-409

Note 1 (All Questions) — Although the regulation named the individuals, it actually applied to anyone, in that it prohibited certain types of transaction with the individuals. Thus it was not plausible to suggest that it only addressed certain individuals, even though the named parties were the ones not directly affected.

Note 2 The basic regulation 896/2001 covered a "closed class" with respect to traditional importers in the sense that there were a finite number of them. However, it was impossible to know exactly who would be affected until applications for reference quantities had been made. The case with respect to Regulation 1121/2001 seemed stronger because by then the precise identity and reference quantities had become known. Moreover, since it set the co-efficient, it had a definitive effect on the actual reference quantities. Nonetheless, the Court concluded that the measure was a regulation because it applied a general rule and did not address individual situations. This seems to be pushing the traditional test for a regulation to the limit. The Court perhaps was reacting to the rather bruising earlier episode where it had been overturned on appeal and was trying to follow what it understood the ECJ's general guidance was. With respect to this latter Regulation it is not at first sight clear that it came to the right conclusion. The measure in question had effects only on a closed class and could easily have been adopted by a decision since it did not need to have a general normative effect. However, the Court was also no doubt influenced by the way the later regulation was simply the final stage of an overall normative structure: it would have been difficult to envisage how a challenge to it would not have upset the overall structure. It is nonetheless questionable whether this ought to be influential in analyzing the legal nature of an act.

[B]   The Characteristics of Directives

GOVERNMENT OF GIBRALTAR v. COUNCIL
Case 298/89, 1993 ECJ CELEX LEXIS 13, [1993] ECR I-3605

Note 1 Although Member States have standing to challenge directives, the UK government had pointed out that the government of Gibraltar was not an authority of a Member State. Only the Governor, acting on the wishes of the UK government itself, constituted a State for this purpose. Thus Gibraltar needed to establish standing as a private individual, which meant it could not seek to annul a directive (see Art 230). [Note changes to article 230 in the Treaty of Lisbon.]

Note 2 The applicant's argument that a specific provision of a directive could be treated as a decision was firmly rejected by the Court. This does not rule out the possibility however that a whole directive could be a disguised decision. The CFI has not ruled out such a possibility. See *Union Europeenne del'artisanat et des petites et moyennes entreprises v. Council* Case T-135/96, 1998 ECJ CELEX LEXIS 144, [1998] ECR II-2335.

CRIMINAL PROCEEDINGS AGAINST SILVIO BERLUSCONI AND OTHERS
Joined Cases C-387/02, C-391/02 and C-403/02, 2005 ECJ CELEX LEXIS 750, [2005]
ECR I-3565

Note 1 Q1 — The underlying principle here is that while an unimplemented directive may be invoked against a Member State, the latter cannot invoke it against individuals. This of course would not apply if the national legislature had opted to enact the directive exactly as drafted with no intermediary legislation (such as the UK essentially did with the Commercial Agents Directive).

Q2 — If the Italian court were to conclude that the directive had not been complied with, its duty would be nonetheless to apply the lesser penalty provided by Italian law. This is somewhat at odds with the concept that the Courts are authorities of the Member States and are bound by Article 10. However, the ECJ clearly wishes to discourage the Member States from inaction; and perhaps more importantly, the principle of legal certainty, also part of the EU legal order, clearly trumps the duty to observe the terms of the directive.

INTER-ENVIRONNEMENT WALLONIE ASBL v. REGION WALLONNE
Case C-129/96, 1997 ECJ CELEX LEXIS 571, [1997] ECR I-7411

Note 1 It should be noted in the first place that there is nothing in Article 249 that requires any, or any particular, transposition period. Hence, as the Court points out, such a period is included only insofar as it is necessary to give Member States time to adopt the implementing measures. In this particular case the Belgian authority had adopted a measure, apparently to implement the directive but allegedly not in conformity with it, before the implementation period had expired. Such action could be considered a violation of Article 10 and therefore is potentially unenforceable. If on the other hand, the law was only one step in a process of implementation, it could be considered as merely transitional and therefore acceptable. Thus, in essence, while in general it remains the case that a directive may only be asserted against a Member State after the implementation date has passed, it is possible that the assertion could occur before such date if the legislation was indeed intended to be the full implementing measure. See also the *Mangold* case set out in Chapter 17, *infra*.

Note 2 (All Questions) — It would follow from the Court's reasoning that mere executive actions under existing law do not need to be consistent with the directive prior to its implementation date. Even a change in national legislation that was not part of the implementation would be permissible; and the national courts are not required to observe the directive's provisions before the deadline.

[C] Framework Decisions

CRIMINAL PROCEEDINGS AGAINST MARIA PUPINO
Case C-105/03, 2005 ECJ CELEX LEXIS 774, [2005] ECR I-5285

[This case is a useful tool for illustrating the differences between the TEU and the EC Treaties regarding instruments and effects.]

Note 1 The various interveners were concerned that by asking the question, the national court was treating the framework decisions as at least capable of producing direct effects — i.e. that it was invocable in the sense used in this book. This is clearly excluded by Article 34(2)(b) TEU. If the Court had jurisdiction to give an interpretation, the national court would be bound to follow it. This then would create a circumvention of Article 34. The Court rejected this argument holding, that it was not its role to determine the relevance of the question to the resolution of the main proceedings.

Note 2 It then pointed out that nonetheless the courts of the Member States have a duty to interpret national law in conformity with the Framework Decision. This clearly falls short of direct effect, since it does not invite the national court to overrule the national law if it is plainly in contradiction of the Decision. It then went on to impose a caveat that an interpretation based on the Framework Decision that led to a change in the criminal liability of an individual without the intermediary of a national law was not permissible. This was not the case here, since the question related to a procedure for taking evidence.

Note 3 The Court referred to the duty of sincere cooperation without referencing specifically article 10 EC. It considered that the duty applied in the context of the TEU just as much as in the EC Treaty. This might seem controversial but at least logical — the two treaties are part of an overall uniform framework. This is reinforced by the Treaty of Lisbon, of course.

Note 4 A framework decision, as pointed out by the Court, has the same kind of legal effect on the Member States as a directive. The only difference is that it cannot produce direct effects. A framework decision is only possible under Article 34(2)(b) — Title VI, Police and Judicial Co-operation in Criminal Matters.

Decisions under Title VI correspond to "decisions" in the EC Treaty, except again that there is no direct effect.

Conventions are only binding on the states that adopt them — Title VI only.

Decisions under Title V (Common Foreign and Security Policy) are binding on the Member States, but the ECJ has no jurisdiction.

Note 5 The national Courts would be bound to ignore any such arguments based on the principle of sincere cooperation, one would think. The supremacy of the TEU and legislative acts under that Treaty has not yet been tested.

[D] Other Acts Having Legal Effects

SOCIETE ANONYME A PARTICIPATION OUVRIERE COMPAGNIE NATIONALE AIR FRANCE v. COMMISSION
Case T-3/93, 1994 ECJ CELEX LEXIS 183. [1994] ECR II-121

Note 1 In competition matters such as the PVC cases, the Commission is required to act by decision, which requires a formal procedure. By contrast, in the case of the merger regulation, the question whether the merger in question is of an EU dimension is based on an objective test and does not require a formal Commission decision to that effect. Thus no particular formality is required. The Court will look only to see whether the Commission's determination changes the legal status of the applicant, which it clearly did because it meant that the merger would not be subject to the Merger Regulation, but rather to national (UK) evaluation only. This change in legal status is the critical element in determining whether the act can be challenged under article 230. This means in effect that the term "decision" as used in that article is not being used in the same way as it is in Article 249, contrary to assertions in other cases that the Treaty ought to be read consistently when using such terms. Compare however the next case, where the CFI clearly held that the act in question was a "decision" despite missing some of the formal requirements.

INFRONT WM AG v. COMMISSION
Case T-33/01, 2005 ECJ CELEX LEXIS 691, [2005] ECR II-5897

Note 1 In this and previous cases, the EU Courts have consistently ruled that any act of an EU institution that changes the legal position of a person or state is a legally binding act that permits it to be reviewed by the EU courts. In this case, the conclusions communicated by the Commission to the UK had the effect of validating the UK's list, thus changing the status of the UK government in that regard by removing an uncertainty about the legality of any action taken by it in implementing its policy based on the list. Article 249 only mentions certain specific instruments, so one might conclude that all "other acts" must be "decisions" — as the CFI did here. But this then does raise the question of how one reconciles cases like *Air France* and *Solvay*. Note that article 230 gives the Court general jurisdiction to review all "acts" of the institutions, though in the case of private challenges its jurisdiction is limited to review of "decisions." Keep in mind the changes in the Treaty of Lisbon in this regard.

REYNOLDS TOBACCO AND OTHERS v. COMMISSION
Case C-131/03, 2006 ECJ CELEX LEXIS 442, [2006] ECR I-7795

Note 1 The Courts' decisions here certainly make sense. Were they to have decided otherwise, the way would have been open to anyone to challenge any internal act of the Institutions to do anything, which could lead to complete paralysis. The actual analysis however is quite interesting and might spark some discussion as to whether in fact the applicants were affected in some way — after all, as a result of the decision arguably they were forced to defend the U.S. actions. This may have meant they were not directly concerned as required by article 230 (see chapter 13) but nonetheless arguably the act produced a legal effect in the abstract.

§ 3.04   JUDICIAL DECISIONS AS A SOURCE OF LAW

[A]   Article 234 Judgments as Precedent

DA COSTA EN SCHAAKE NV, JACOB MEIJER NV, HOECHST-HOLLAND NV v. NETHERLANDS INLAND REVENUE ADMINISTRATION
Joined Cases 28-30/62, [1963] ECR 31

Note 2 Q1 — The ECJ approached the issue obliquely, referring to its explicit duty under Article 234. As will be seen in Chapter 15, it *may* be prepared to decline to hear a case where the reference is a result of a contrived lawsuit or has some purpose beyond that of giving guidance to the national court; but it will accept jurisdiction otherwise, even in a clear case where it has answered the exact same question. Of course, the national court might well decide in such a case that no reference is necessary — see for example the *Cohn-Bendit* decision in the previous chapter.

So far as original jurisdiction is concerned, it is the practice today of both the CFI and ECJ to cite prior decisions, as will have already been seen in cases in this chapter. However, the courts do not state that they consider themselves "bound" by those prior decisions as a matter of law, and indeed, as will be seen in Chapter 14 (*UPA* and *Jégo Quéré*) the CFI has occasionally attempted to change an approach which had become well entrenched (*i.e.* the notion of direct and individual concern in Article 230).

Q2 and Q3 — Overall, however, there is a marked contrast with the common law approach to decided cases. Common lawyers are used to reviews of possibly conflicting precedent where it is necessary to elicit the *ratio decidendi* that constitutes the binding core and then if necessary distinguish the case at hand. The ECJ and CFI on the other hand seek generally to rationalize *ex lege* in a logical flow from the general to the particular, with an underlying premise that all the law is actually to be found in the Treaties ("Code") and EU legislation. This surely is the opposite of the traditional common law, where the cases *are* the law.

[B]   Interpretative Techniques

BULMER v. BOLLINGER
(Denning MR)
[1974] Ch. 401

Note 1 Recourse to the decision of courts in other Member States is not really a necessary component of the process. That is what Article 234 is supposed to avoid. If there is any doubt about the interpretation of an EU law, a national court should not take on itself the task of deriving a meaning from all the various jurisdictions.

Note 2 As has already become evident from cases such as *Simmenthal* and *Factortame*, the national courts are under an obligation to set aside any procedural rule that would interfere with the application of EU law. The dilemma posed here is analogous to the situation that had prevailed in Italy prior to the *Granital* case where the ordinary courts were not permitted to question the validity of legislation.

Note 3 At first glance the various approaches and analyses here seem to be mutually contradictory or even to cancel each other out to the point that no interpretative technique emerges: if one argues that no recourse to intention is possible, but also that the interpretation must be focused on the future (teleological), what is left? In fact, the case law of the EU Courts very clearly demonstrates that interpretation is based on the underlying stated objectives in the Treaties themselves. This is abundantly clear from the earlier cases such as *Costa v. ENEL*. This allows for an approach where the Treaties become a self-contained system of law, supporting, then, both a document specific yet teleological approach.

Chapter 4

INTERACTION OF THE EU AND INTERNATIONAL LEGAL SYSTEMS

§ 4.02 ISSUES ARISING FROM THE STATUS OF THE MEMBER STATES AS CONTINUING SUBJECTS OF INTERNATIONAL LAW

[A] The Application of General Principles of Customary International Law to the Interpretation and Effects of the Treaties

COMMISSION v. LUXEMBOURG AND BELGIUM
(MILK PRODUCTS)
Joined Cases 90, 91/63, [1964] ECR 625

COMMISSION v. FRANCE
(MUTTON AND LAMB)
Case 232/78, [1979] ECR 2729

Note 1 The court did not reject the proposition that international law principles could play a role in the relationships established by the EC Treaty. However, the principle raised in both cases, that of the condition of reciprocity between contracting states in the observance of treaty obligations, could play no part in the new legal order. Occasionally the court does refer to international law — see as a further example the *Foglia v. Novello* cases in chapter 15, regarding the propriety of calling into question the laws of another Member State. The overall answer then is that international law is still relevant but is heavily circumscribed by the nature of the EU legal order.

Note 2 The statement seems accurate. The EC treaty, particularly as it has developed over 50 years contains its own inbuilt interpretative techniques that largely are self-contained. Thus was not true of the ECSC Treaty.

[B] Effects of the Treaties on Continuing Treaty Relations Between the Member States and Third Countries

BUDEJOVICKY BUDVAR, NARODN I PODNIK v. RUDOLF AMMERSIN GMBH
Case C-216/01, 2003 ECJ CELEX LEXIS 399, [2003] ECR I-13617

Note 1 (Both questions) — Article 307 EC expressly permits the continuation of pre-existing treaty obligations subject to the proviso that, so far as possible, they should be construed so as to not place the Member State in a position where it would otherwise be in breach of Treaty obligations. It does however impose a duty to remove the incompatibilities and this is reinforced by the duty owed by the Member States to fellow States arising from the advantages it has received and the transfer of competence it has agreed to. In this case, the issue was complicated by the fact that Czechoslovakia had broken up and it seems to follow that to the extent that Austria had the freedom to choose not to be bound by the convention in question vis-à-vis the Czech Republic, it should have chosen not to be. Conceivably, a failure to exercise this option might itself have been a breach of the EC Treaty. To that extent the resolution of the question was no longer an Austrian, but an EU issue.

AHMED ALI YUSUF AND AL BARAKAAT INTERNATIONAL FOUNDATION v. COUNCIL AND COMMISSION
Case T-306/01, 2005 ECJ CELEX LEXIS 422, [2005] ECR II 3533

Note 1 The court did not apply any form of succession doctrine here (see para 242). Instead, following cases such as *Poulsen* (later in this chapter), it took a purely pragmatic approach. It determined that the EC treaty had expressly reserved the obligations of the *Member States* under international treaties, such that the Member States themselves continue to be responsible for compliance with the UN charter and the actions of the Security Council.

Note 2 Any action requiring the involvement of the EU pursuant to the transfer of internal powers or the obligations of the Member States would have to be expressly subject to the pre-existing UN duties. The issues here would not arise in the US because the various states are not subjects of international law — only the U.S can play such a role.

Note 3 It is very clear from the judgment that the CFI did not consider that the EU principles relating to fundamental rights could be applied to the internal legislation implementing the U.N Security Council resolutions, because this would impede the Member States' ability to comply with them. However, it considered that the UN actions themselves were subject to fundamental rights principles that formed part of the "*ius cogens*" to which international law was subject. Thus the court was willing to analyze the applicants' arguments in relation to that law, but not EU law. It is interesting to speculate on what would happen if the *ius cogens* did not coincide with EU principles — a sort of parallel on the international level with the EU/Germany case law — *Internationale Handelsgesellschaft* and *Brunner*. In fact, this was almost the case with respect to the CFI's analysis of the right to be heard. In EU law, such a right would exist in relation to legislation affecting a person directly and individually, while this was not so with respect to the UN action. It managed to finesse the issue by considering that the Sanctions Committee procedure, while not permitting a court action, did contain safeguards that met the requirements of ius cogens in the circumstances.

Note 4 Q1/2 — The CFI uses the Universal Declaration of Human Rights as a source and also somewhat makes use of principles developed within the EU system. Perhaps the former is at least an indicator of human rights principles at least within the "closed system" of the United Nations Charter, but it is not established that it is part of *ius cogens* in the general body of international law. References to EU principles contradicts the notion perhaps that this also is a unique legal order that is not any longer in the realm of international law (though one recalls the words of the ECJ in *Costa*, that is a new legal order international law). Altogether the reasoning seems a little self serving and does not take account of the vast body of literature and learning on the subject.

Q3 — One could criticize the CFI for not seeking expert evidence on the question of *ius cogens*, if one accepts that international law and EU law are not the same legal systems, just as one would obtain expert evidence on a foreign legal question in a domestic court. One could argue of course that EU law is still a variant of international law in which case the judges could be said to be deciding issues within their own legal system. This is really a very interesting question to which there seems to be no clear answer (yet).

Q4 — This is the most difficult question of all here: surely the CFI would not be competent to determine that the Security Council Sanctions committee had breached international law? In practical terms it would of course have no power to annul such a decision, but would nonetheless then have to find that EU law should be invoked to annul the EU action, thus potentially putting the Member States in violation of their UN obligations. Thus indirectly the CFI would have meddled in UN matters. Presumably the Member States would then have to ask the Sanctions Committee to revise its procedures and re-adopt its decisions in compliance with the rights determined by the CFI. Fortunately this did not happen but the CFI is clearly in dangerous waters here.

[C] Effects of the EU and EC Treaties on Other Treaty Relationships Between the Member States

SOCIETA ITALIANA PER L'OLEODOTTO TRANSALPINO (SIOT) v. MINISTERO DELLE FINANZE, MINISTERO DELLA MARINA MERCANTILE
Case 266/81, 1983 ECJ CELEX LEXIS 50, [1983] ECR731

Note 2 The question regarding the application of GATT arose from the ambiguity of the Treaty provisions on the issue as to whether they applied to goods in transit. Had they not done so, it is arguable that the EU could not have been considered a customs union within the sense of Article XXIV GATT and this would have caused the entire EU structure to have been invalid due to the discriminations that would then exist between the Member States' treatment of each other (with the complete elimination of customs duties) and their treatment of other states, where tariffs could still be imposed. The Court thus considered that GATT continued to bind the Member States, since otherwise it would not have been necessary to invoke Article XXIV GATT. But it is clear that their obligations ceased under GATT as among themselves by virtue of that Article.

COMMISSION v. IRELAND
(NUCLEAR REPROCESSING)
Case C-459/03, 2006 ECJ CELEX LEXIS 238, [2006] ECR I-04635

Note 2 The issues in this case have close connections with the issues that arose in the EEA Opinions (chapter 3) in that the ECJ examined Ireland's conduct in light of the threats to the autonomy of the EU legal order and its own exclusive jurisdiction to hear disputes between Member States relating to any matter of EU law.

The following principles may be discerned from the judgment:

First, the underlying convention here was a mixed agreement, that is, it involved commitments that implicated both EU and Member States competences. The ECJ indicated that such agreements have the same status as agreements falling within the EU's exclusive competence and thus it is the duty of the Member States under article 10 EC to ensure respect for those commitments.

Second, any dispute concerning the interpretation of the EC Treaty or secondary legislation must be decided by the ECJ per article 292 EC. Any reference to another tribunal of questions involving even potentially the interpretation of EU rules is unacceptable.

Third, any question regarding whether or not a matter is within the scope of the EC Treaty and EU competence must be decided by the ECJ. It is not up to the Member States to make this determination.

Fourth, while it is not the case that the EU alone has the right to bring proceedings in another tribunal where the case relates solely to subject matter within the competence of the Member States, in any mixed agreement there remains a duty to consult with the Commission because of the possible effects on EU law. (See further Chapter 11, *infra*.)

Note 3 (All questions) — The duty under Article 10 EC would at least require the Member State to examine whether it has any duty to consult with the Commission. In the examples used, there would be EU issues affected, even if somewhat remotely. As the EU scope of competence continues to expand, even in areas where the EU has no power to legislate as such, it seems logical to expect a point to be reached where all international disputes involving two or more Member States will require some sort of interaction with or intervention by, the Commission.

§ 4.03   INTERNATIONAL LAW IN THE EU LEGAL SYSTEM

[A]   Assumption of Pre-Existing Treaty Obligations

INTERNATIONAL FRUIT CO. NV v. PRODUKTSCHAP VOOR GROENTEN EN FRUIT
Joined Cases 21–22/72, [1972] ECR 1219

Note 1 (Both questions) — The Court's response indicates that the GATT binds the EU because of the transfer of competence in commercial policy from the Member States. Thus, the court does not apply any general doctrine of international law regarding the succession of obligations. This is purely a matter of EU law. Had any of the contracting parties to GATT refused to recognize the role of the EU, the Member States would have been duty bound under article 10 to take whatever measures the EU might refuse to assure that, at least internally, the EU powers would not be compromised.

[B]   Internal EU Legal Effects of Treaties Entered into by the EU

GERMANY v. COUNCIL
(BANANAS)
Case C-280/93, 1994 ECJ CELEX LEXIS 385, [1994] ECR I-4973

Note 1 (All questions) — It is worth noting that the court could not adopt the same rationale as it had when considering EC Treaty provisions, because there was no surrender of sovereign rights under GATT. The court simply analyzed the nature of the provisions to determine whether they were capable of being involved, perhaps similar to the way the U.S courts might look at a U.S treaty obligation. The criteria seem to be entirely a matter for EU law. The approach could be considered a pure manifestation of the dualist approach. In essence, the express incorporation by reference into an EU regulation turns the GATT provision into a part of EU domestic law.

Note 3 The national court would have to start from the premise that EU law takes precedence. However, it could also conclude that the EU did not intend to enact legislation contrary.to the obligations of the Member States. If that were impossible, then perhaps the court could fall back on the principle of Article 307 that the EC Treaty did not affect pre-existing treaty obligations. Thus the role of EU law, being subsidiary to the EC Treaty, would have to yield to the overriding Treaty provisions.

Note 5 (All questions) — The entry into force of an international agreement through the EU ratification process is enough to give it legal force. The EU thus has a purely dualist system. Admittedly, the execution of a treaty requires a Council decision and in some cases approval by the Parliament, but this corresponds to ratification rather than incorporation. Furthermore, as a practical matter, it is usually necessary to adopt regulations in implementation of the Treaty. But this should not be allowed to obscure the underlying doctrinal approach.

Note 6 Once a treaty has become part of EU law, it can be invoked by individuals where a provision has direct effect, regardless of whether or not the subject matter lies within the competence of the Member States, since it is impossible to segment it based on the division of competences. This seems to follow also from the *Ireland* case, *supra*, and from the effect of article 10.

[C] Role of Customary International Law and International Conventions in the EU Legal System

A. RACKE GMBH & CO. v. HAUPTZOLLAMT MAINZ
Case 162/96, 1998 ECJ CELEX LEXIS 280, [1998] ECR I-3655

Note 1 (Both questions) — The Court considered that the EU was bound by customary international law. As such any rule made by the authorities could be reviewed to discover whether it was in breach of international law in the same way as it could for compliance with fundamental rights. In this case however, there was no breach of the rule of international law alleged by the applicants relating to the principle that agreements should be observed, because it was an implicit term of the agreement that it could be suspended if the Yugoslavian cease-fire were not observed.

ANKLAGEMYNDIGHEDEN v. PETER MICHAEL POULSEN AND DIVA NAVIGATION CORP.
Case C-286/90, 1992 ECJ CELEX LEXIS 197, [1992] ECR I-6019

Note 1 The Court simply made the statement without any explanation, presumably because it was considered too obvious to require any further rationale. In fact the Court could have referred to Article 220. It could also have pointed out that the Member States were all bound by international law and therefore could not have surrendered more power to the EU than they themselves possessed. The point is expressly made in the *Yusuf* case, above. One can speculate however that sooner or later this approach might give rise to problems: for example if Member States followed different interpretations of the Treaty-laws such as the Conventions at issue here; or some were parties to a convention while others were not. In that case one would wonder which version of the international rule binds the EU.

Note 2 (All questions) — The final leg in the argument of the applicants was that they and their cargo were protected by the law relating to vessels in distress. The court considered that to be a question for the Danish court. Quite conceivably the views of national courts in the various Member States could differ on the scope and meaning of this doctrine.

There is clearly a potential for differences in application from one state to another based on whether international law principles have direct effect and thus there might be some inconsistency of application. At any rate, in the view of the Court, this remained a national law question. Of course, the Danish court would be bound to take account of article 10, so as to ensure that the national law or view of international law within the Danish system did not impede the effect of the EU regulation. But so far as the ECJ was concerned, it seems whatever result arose from Danish law would be consistent with EU law.

Part III
LEGISLATIVE COMPETENCES

Chapter 5

LEGISLATIVE COMPETENCES — GENERAL THEMES

§ 5.02 RELATIONSHIP BETWEEN COMPETENCES IN THE EU AND EC TREATIES

COMMISSION v. COUNCIL
(CRIMINAL PENALTIES FOR ENVIRONMENTAL OFFENCES)
Case 176/03, 2005 ECJ CELEX LEXIS 754, [2005] ECR I-7879

Note 1 The ECJ based its conclusion on the underlying scope of the EC Treaty. The Treaty covers matters relating to the internal market and the environment. In this case, the legislation was an aspect of the environmental policies of the EU and indeed had the potential to affect them in several ways. There was nothing in the EC Treaty that suggested the EU could not require the imposition of criminal penalties. The advantage from the Member States' point of view in trying to adopt this legislation under the TEU was that it was not directly effective; and it could be adopted on the proposal of a Member State, while under the EC Treaty a Commission proposal would have been necessary.

>From a broader perspective, the ECJ's approach suggests that it will look beyond any specific wording to the general scope and intent of the EC Treaty, which is the only document that it is able to interpret. It has no jurisdiction to interpret the EU treaty on this subject. Hence if the Member States or the Council took a different view, there is no ready method for resolving the conflict other than to conclude that the terms of the EC Treaty will prevail.

§ 5.03 DIVISION OF COMPETENCES BETWEEN THE EU AND THE MEMBER STATES

[A] EU Exclusive Powers

LIEUTENANT COMMANDER A. G. ROGERS v. H. B. L. DARTHENAY
Case 87/82, [1983] ECR 1579

Note 1 The UK/Denmark/Ireland Act of Accession had prescribed that the (then) Community would assume full responsibility for fisheries from the end of the transitional period. The Community had then adopted a general scheme but had not yet adopted the detailed rules. The Court was concerned to establish the point that it would be unacceptable for individual Member States to take "Member State action" which could jeopardize the common organization.

Note 2 There seems no reason why the national court could not look to the UK legislation as guidance as to what the "supplementary rules" might ultimately look like. However the court was not permitted to apply the statutory instrument as such since it contained provisions that were not acceptable to the EU.

[B]   The Scope of Harmonization Powers

GERMANY v. PARLIAMENT AND COUNCIL
(TOBACCO ADVERTISING)
Case C-376/98, 2000 ECJ CELEX LEXIS 366 [2000] ECR I-8419

Note 1 The Court's analysis is a masterpiece of legal reasoning brought to bear on a very difficult subject. The logic goes as follows:

(a)   Article 152 precludes harmonization of health measures which remain firmly in the control of the Member States.

(b)   Article 95 requires that harmonization be based on the need to eliminate distortions arising from differing Member State legislation take into account the need for a high level of protection of human health, but this is not its permitted objective, rather it is the standard for the policy choices as to the type of rules that will be used to standardize the legislation.

(c)   The only products that would be considered to be the valid subject of harmonization here would be the media and advertisements of tobacco products.

(d)   It is necessary therefore to ascertain whether the directive removes obstacles to trade in such "products".

(e)   Since the advertising is mostly local, by and large there is no obstacle to "trade" — the advertising does not move between Member States.

(f)   Moreover, the directive contains provisions which make trade in these products more difficult because Member States can actually lay down stricter measures for banning tobacco advertising.

(g)   There is no requisite distortion of competition.

(h)   The ban on advertising makes trade more difficult and therefore actually increases the risk of distortion.

Note 2 The Member States could have taken individual action as long as they did not prejudice the fundamental freedoms. This was not an area where they had been preempted.

[C]   Preemptive Effects of Harmonization

COMMISSION v. UNITED KINGDOM
(DIM — DIP)
Case 60/86, 1988 ECJ CELEX LEXIS 120, [1988] ECR 3921

PUBBLICO MINISTERO v. RATTI
Case 148/78, [1979] ECR 1629

MINISTERE PUBLIC v. GRUNERT
Case 88/79, [1980] ECR 1827

Note 1 In the D*im-dip* case the Court traced the ancestry of Directive 76/156 and concluded that it was one of many directives intended to lay down exhaustive provisions regarding its subject matter. The UK argument by contrast was based on any extremely narrow interpretation that was essentially circuitous. If the directive was intended to be exhaustive as to rules relating to lighting and signaling devices, an argument that "these devices" meant that it did not exclude others not specifically mentioned was clearly erroneous. It is also an interesting reflection on how the classic literal interpretation approach to statutory construction is not tenable in the context of an EU directive — especially since such an interpretation technique would not be used in other systems or languages.

The differences in approach and degree to which Member States are permitted continued freedom of action are explained by the stage of harmonization reflected in the directive. It will be evident from these cases. This can range from complete exclusion to mere high-level principles.

Note 2 As will be evident from Chapters 6 and 7, the Court's interpretation of articles EC 28 and 49 in particular may be pushing the Member States towards mutual recognition that could lead to a general lowering of standards as well as abuse. (This is discussed at length in Chapter 6).

[D]   Conferral of Responsibilities on the EU in the Context of Harmonized Laws

GERMANY v. COUNCIL
(CONSUMER PRODUCT SAFETY)
Case 359/92, 1994 ECJ CELEX LEXIS 138, [1994] ECR I-3681

Note 1 (All questions) — Article 95 was introduced as a supplement to Article 94, which specifies directives as the means of approximation, or harmonization, of Member States' laws. Clearly Article 95 was intended to go further by, first of all, expanding the scope of EU action to laws that did not "directly affect" the establishment or functioning of the common market. The German argument was that Article 9 of the directive, which contemplated action by the Commission going beyond mere harmonization, could not qualify as a "measure for the approximation of the [Member States' laws]". The Court rejected this interpretation: and it is worth noting of course that Article 95 specifically does *not* confine itself to directives.

Note 2 Harmonization is a very imperfect approach if it is confined strictly to the alignment of the laws of the Member States. Instead, a more flexible approach is needed, reflecting the reality that harmonization is not a neutral process — inevitably choices of policy have to be made and where some flexibility is permitted the Commission must be permitted the power to monitor for consistency with the principles adopted.

[E]   Subsidiarity and Proportionality

COMMISSION REPORT TO THE EUROPEAN COUNCIL ENTITLED 'BETTER LAWMAKING 2001' (PURSUANT TO ARTICLE 9 OF THE EC TREATY PROTOCOL ON THE APPLICATION OF THE PRINCIPLES OF SUBSIDIARITY AND PROPORTIONALITY)
Bulletin EU 12-2001
Institutional Questions and the Future of the Union (7/9)
[COM (2001) 728]

THE TREATY OF AMSTERDAM PROTOCOL ON THE APPLICATION OF THE PRINCIPLES OF SUBSIDIARITY AND PROPORTIONALITY
THE "LAEKEN DECLARATION" OF DEC 14/15 2001

Note 2 As the following cases indicate, the ECJ is certainly willing to consider whether the subsidiarity principle has been breached. However, it has yet to make such a finding, and this is perhaps not surprising since every legislative act must contain a statement of reasons and these will include a recitation of the grounds as to why it is necessary for the EU to act. It is difficult to imagine circumstances where the Court would find that these grounds were incorrect. Thus, it is really at the stage prior to adoption of legislation that the debate occurs as to whether EU action is necessary. That is clearly a political decision.

Note 3 This question would arise where a national court decided to apply a national law that was contrary to EU law and concluded that the EU law was invalid for breach of the principle. The ECJ has made it clear that national courts are not permitted to determine the validity of EU legislation. (See Chapter 15, *infra*). Thus, such a matter would necessarily be ruled on only by the EU Courts, and for the reasons stated above, it is most unlikely that the EU law could be invalidated on that ground.

Note 4 (All questions) — This proposal would have inserted the courts into the legislative process. It seems hard to imagine how the court could have played such a role, since it could only really evaluate the legislation once it was in final form, and thus would then raise the same issue described in Note 2 above. To ask the Court to intervene at an earlier stage would have created a politicized situation, which would not have been appropriate for a court. The Court has also strenuously resisted attempts to give it advisory as opposed to decisional powers. Thus, in terms of what this proposal contemplated, it was not feasible and was wisely abandoned.

Note 5 Subsidiarity addresses the question: is it appropriate for the EU to take action? The Proportionality principle applies once the first question has been affirmatively answered. Thus it goes to the issue of the degree and nature of the regulation proposed. The following cases illustrate this difference.

UNITED KINGDOM v. COUNCIL
(WORKING TIME DIRECTIVE)
Case C-84/94, 1996 ECJ CELEX LEXIS 194, [1996] ECR I-5755

Note 1 (All questions) — The UK's arguments were founded on the premise that it was possible to offer alternatives to the measures in issue that would achieve the same goal. The ECJ rejected such arguments based on an approach that defers to the Council's exercise of discretion in discussing a particular solution and declines any independent evaluation except in the case of "manifest error". This notion would only come into play where the statement of reasons or rationale given by the Council was mistaken on its face — as, for example, a fatal flaw in a logical argument or reliance on a fundamentally erroneous statistic. The approach is very similar to that which the court had adopted in other areas relating to the exercise of discretion (see Chapter 14, *infra*).

Note 2 Given the degree of latitude allowed, it seems highly unlikely that proportionality arguments will succeed.

GERMANY v. PARLIAMENT AND COUNCIL
(DEPOSIT GUARANTEE SCHEME)
Case C-233/94, 1997 ECJ CELEX LEXIS 55, [1997] ECR I-2405

Note 1 The interesting phenomenon in this case is that it highlights two different aspects of proportionality. The first has to do with the legislative choices as to the means of achieving the objectives of the legislature. The second has to do with the more specific issue as to whether the requirements impose a burden on the addressees of the legislation that causes an undue burden to be imposed on them. In other words, this is a variant of the principle that the penalty for the breach of a rule should be proportionate to its goals (see Chapter 17, *infra*).

THE QUEEN v. SECRETARY OF STATE FOR HEALTH, EX PARTE BRITISH AMERICAN TOBACCO (INVESTMENTS) LTD AND IMPERIAL TOBACCO LTD
Case C-491/01, 2002 ECJ CELEX LEXIS 628, [2002] ECR I-11453

Note 1 The argument would clearly strip the nation of subsidiarity of its central purpose. If internal market measures are not covered at all, it would be possible to adopt any measure at the EU level simply by finding some basis, however remote, that the internal market was affected. In practice, though, this seems to be exactly what the ECJ is doing in these cases. The reference to "exclusive competence" in Article 5 EC is also confusing since the Treaty does not otherwise define what areas are in that category. Some guidance is available from the Court (see the following chapters, especially 8 and 10) but without a definition, why would it not be possible to argue that internal market harmonization is a matter of exclusive EU competence? Altogether, the subsidiarity principle is difficult to pin down from a legal point of view. Once again, it really only works from a political standpoint.

§ 5.04   TREATY LIMITATIONS, IMPLIED POWERS AND THE ROLE OF ARTICLE 308

GERMANY v. COMMISSION
(ARTICLE 137)

Joined Cases 281, 283–285 and 287/85, 1987 ECJ CELEX LEXIS 191, [1987] ECR 3203

Note 1 (All questions) — The central issue of concern to the Member States was that the Commission had used Article 137 to determine and direct Member States' actions in the area of social policy when the Article itself only permits consultations. It could be viewed perhaps as an attempt to by-pass the Article 226 procedure to some degree, though this ultimately would be the appropriate course of action to follow if indeed a Member State action were to impede the functioning of the internal market or other EU competences. It is relatively unusual for the Court to deny appropriate powers for the implementation of EC Treaty provisions. The Court's objection is thus perhaps surprising and may reflect a recognition of the strength of the objections voiced by the applicants.

Note 2 The Council could have taken action under Article 308 but this seems unlikely given the objections raised. It is conceivable that Articles 95 or 96 also could have been invoked, but again, action by the Council would be required.

SPAIN v. COUNCIL
(PATENTS FOR MEDICINAL PRODUCTS)

Case C-350/92, 1995 ECJ CELEX LEXIS 38, [1995] ECR I-1985

Note 1 (Both questions) — The Spanish government had tried to argue that Articles 30 and 295 expressly limit the powers of the EU in the field of intellectual property. This was implicit through the wording of Articles 30 and 295. The ECJ, however, upheld the regulation based on Article 95 (not included in the extract) and in doing so concluded that the cited articles did not narrow EU competence. The case therefore does not really support a notion of implied powers in EU domestic legislation.

COMMISSION v. COUNCIL
(ERASMUS)

Case 242/87, 1989 ECJ CELEX LEXIS 413, [1989] ECR 1425

Note 1 At first blush the "necessary and proper" clause of the U.S. Constitution and article 308 of the EC Treaty appear to differ greatly from one another. The necessary and proper clause, after all, expressly limits the power of Congress "to make all Laws which shall be necessary and proper for carrying into Execution the *foregoing powers* and *all other powers vested by this Constitution* in the Government of the United States, or in any Department or Officer thereof." (emphasis supplied) By contrast article 308 of the EC Treaty expressly allows the Council to "take the appropriate measures" where the Treaty has *not* provided the necessary powers. In practice, however, and in light of interpretations by the ECJ and the U.S. Supreme Court, this difference is more apparent than real.

Note 3 Given the Court's views expressed in *Opinion 2/94 (Accession to the ECHR)* mentioned in note 2, it seems unlikely that Article 308 could be used in such circumstances.

Chapter 6

REGULATION OF THE MARKETING AND SALE OF GOODS

§ 6.02 GENERAL PRINCIPLES

[A] Scope of Article 28

PROCUREUR DU ROI v. BENOIT AND GUSTAVE DASSONVILLE
Case 8/74, [1974] ECR 837

Note 1 (All questions) — The *Dassonville* decision is extraordinarily broad. The Court refers to "any trading rules which are capable of hindering directly or indirectly, actually or potentially, intra-Community trade . . . ". The restriction here had the effect of making imports of Scotch whisky more difficult if coming from a country other than the UK because the exporter was not able to supply the required certificate. The language quoted above appears at first sight to be broader than what was strictly necessary for the decision, because the restriction here actually addressed imports directly. However, it was, at the same time, a measure that was intended to assure the authenticity of the product. It was not *per se* directed at *restricting* imports. It was therefore necessary for the court to emphasize that the prohibition applied to any measure that might hinder imports, including altering the pattern of trade by making it more difficult to import from one Member State as opposed to another.

[B] Non-discriminatory Rules that Affect Inter-State Trade

REWE — ZENTRAL AG v. BUNDESMONOPOLVERWALTUNG FÜR BRANNTWEIN
("CASSIS DE DIJON")
Case 120/78, [1979] ECR 649

Note 1 Q1 — This would seem logical, but the German Government had actually amended its rules to remove the previously applicable import monopoly and permission requirements, so a clear distinction had been drawn between importation and sale at the retail level. Hence it was not really open to the Court to find that there was still an import restriction.

Q2 — Although the definition given in *Dassonville* was broad enough to cover non-discriminatory provisions, it did not specifically address the situation where a Member State applied an internal law that was on its face non-discriminatory. Hence the *Cassis* case clarified that article 28 did apply in such cases. Thus, while it clarified the definition in *Dassonville*, *Cassis* may be viewed as narrowing the scope of *Dassonville* by introducing certain criteria to judge whether rules otherwise falling within the court's broad language could nonetheless be upheld because they pursue a legitimate purpose.

Q3 — The Court was explicit about the term "produced and marketed" but seems to have subsequently accepted that goods that are simply marketed in another Member State can also benefit — see the *Leclerc* case *infra*, where books had been exported from France and then re-imported. This means then that goods imported from outside the EU could benefit from the ruling, as long as they are lawfully marketed in another Member State first (and not just for the purpose of taking advantage of the ruling.)

Q4 — Since article 28 is only concerned with movement and not production, and thus with goods placed in circulation, the relaxation of the "produced" requirement does not seem to materially alter the scope of its application.

Q5 — In *Cassis*, the Court, after explaining the grounds on which a national rule might be justified notwithstanding an adverse effect on trade, then analyzed how the rule in question should be viewed against those criteria. It doubted that either the public health goal or the consumer protection goals were really legitimate, since the internal German rules and practice seemed themselves to contradict the basic premises alleged by Germany. The Court then noted that (even if the goal of consumer protection were legitimate) it would have been possible to protect the public through adequate labeling. This rather cryptic comment is really a reference to the unstated assumption in the Court's decision that at some level, the national rule must be proportionate to its goal. This then would overcome the "race to the bottom" concern, since each state would be allowed to maintain rules that did indeed serve a legitimate purpose even if this meant that products put in circulation elsewhere were subject to a lower standard, but only as long as the importing state's rule is proportionate to the purpose.

[C] Abuse

ASSOCIATION DES CENTRES DISTRIBUTEURS EDOUARD LECLERC v. "AU BLE VERT" SARL
Case 229/83, 1985 ECJ CELEX LEXIS 95, [1985] ECR

Note 1 Q1 — The ECJ concluded that use of EU law specifically to circumvent national legislation would not be permitted. Thus, the export of a product and its "placing on the market" in another Member State must constitute a genuine attempt to sell such products in the latter state and not simply a device for re-importing the product without compliance with the importing state's rules. From this it must also follow that it is not likely to be possible to apply *Cassis* to wholly internal situations. This is consistent with a strict interpretation of the *Cassis* doctrine which requires only that products lawfully marketed in one Member State may not be subject to stricter or different regulation in another Member State unless such regulation if justified on one of the policy grounds specified by the Court.

Q2 — The Court gave no guidance at all on this. In most cases, it may be clear from the facts that a party is using the free movement provisions for what is really an internal transaction. One could speculate whether for example the appointment of a master distributor for the EU in a country not operating a strict standard for a given product is an abuse — if the distributor then resells to a country that has a higher standard.

[D] The Article 30 Exception

ADRIAAN DE PEIJPER, MANAGING DIRECTOR OF CENTRAFARM BV
Case 104/75, [1976] ECR 613

Note 1 (All questions) — The Court was probably reluctant to consider the Dutch rules as amounting to a disguised restriction on trade or as arbitrarily discriminatory since there was clearly a colorable public health motivation here (unlike *Cassis*). It chose instead to evaluate the rules based on whether or not such measures were indispensable to protecting public health, and whether it was possible to find a less restrictive approach. Moreover, steps taken to encourage parallel imports could actually promote the public health goals by making medicines more accessible at cheaper prices. In effect, then, the Court seems to have applied much the same evaluative criteria as it did in the *Cassis* situation. (Note that *De Peijper* preceded *Cassis*.) Having concluded that the rules were excessive, the Court obviously did not consider it necessary to take the additional analytical step regarding the provisos in Article 30.

Note 2 What would have been objectionable here was the opportunity granted to manufacturers to refuse documentation, where the government was perfectly capable of insisting on their compliance with rules forcing them to do so. It does not seem that the Court was focused on any particular concern that the manufacturers themselves were likely to behave in an abusive way.

COMMISSION v. FRANCE
(IMPORTED MILK POWDER)
Case 216/84, 1988 ECJ CELEX LEXIS 3, [1988] ECR 793

Note 1 Q1 — No the court seems to have blended articles 28 and 30 into a single composite.

Q2 — No — for the same reason.

R. v. MAURICE DONALD HENN AND JOHN FREDERICK ERNEST DARBY
Case 34/79, 1980 ECJ CELEX LEXIS 130, [1979] ECR 3795

Note 1 Q1 — The application of differing standards within a Member State raises the question as to whether there is a genuine morality purpose behind the ban on imports. The U.K. approach to imports essentially chose to apply a specific standard that in a sense was just another standard among the various ones in effect for various parts of the country.

Q2 — The absence of *any* domestic law might seem to be fatal to any bona fide argument that the purpose of the law was the protection of public morality. However, there would at the same time not appear to be any other rationale for this particular restriction. In that case it would be necessary to revert to the provisos regarding disguised restrictions on trade or arbitrary discrimination. A finding to that effect would suggest that the measure was purely protectionist — in other words that the law was actually designed to promote British products in this industry. This obviously would completely undermine the argument that the law was intended to promote public morality. Altogether it becomes rather difficult then to understand why this wouldn't be part of the initial analysis as to the genuine and proportionate purpose of the law.

§ 6.03   SPECIFIC TYPES OF RULES

[A]   Rules that Create an Extra Burden for Imports — the Doctrine of Mutual Recognition

CRIMINAL PROCEEDINGS AGAINST JACQUELINE BRANDSMA
Case C-293/94, 1996 ECJ CELEX LEXIS 262, [1996] ECR I-3159

Note 1 The Court has assiduously sought to avoid the implication that the *Cassis* doctrine entails, in the field of technical standards, a "race to the bottom" by repeatedly asserting the right of the importing state to apply its rules. At the same time it has also suggested that a violation of article 28 will occur where the importing state has not accorded due weight to the qualifications of the product in its state of origin. For this to make sense, there would have surely to be some form of regulation in the latter state. Perhaps however in a case where there is no regulation at all, one would look to general practices to determine whether the regulation in the importing state is an aberration or not. Underlying the whole approach is clearly the desire to ensure that products do not carry a dual burden of regulation.

COMMISSION INTERPRETATIVE COMMUNICATION ON FACILITATING THE ACCESS OF PRODUCTS TO THE MARKETS OF OTHER MEMBER STATES: THE PRACTICAL APPLICATION OF MUTUAL RECOGNITION
([2003] OJ C 265/02)

Note 1 (All questions) — The procedures seem very complex and expensive. It is hard to imagine except in the case of large enterprises, how they could really be an improvement over simply obtaining approval from each destination state. If there is no equivalent requirement in the state of origin, it is difficult to see how the choice of that state not to regulate can be considered equivalent to the regulation required in the destination state. Moreover, in such a case there would not be a double burden on the importer, so perhaps the application of the importing state's rules would not be objectionable.

[B] Rules Applying to a Wholly Internal Situation

TORFAEN BOROUGH COUNCIL v. B & Q PLC
Case C-145/88, 1989 ECJ CELEX LEXIS 357, [1989] ECR 3851

Note 1 — The Court used the *Cassis* logic in principle, but did not see the need itself to undertake any examination of the objective justification for the law (other than to observe that it reflected local cultural and social choices), nor whether it was disproportionate to its goal. Instead, it alluded to Commission directive 70/50 and the reference there to intrinsic effects. It then left it up to the national court to determine whether the law exceeded those effects. It is not surprising that this was read as an invitation for the evaluation of almost any domestic law that could affect the volume of interstate trade. Subsequently, in the *Keck* case, *infra*, the Court, addressing a general trading law that actually could have applied directly to imports, announced a new approach to dealing with laws of this kind.

CRIMINAL   PROCEEDINGS   AGAINST   JACQUES   PISTRE,   MICHELE BARTHES), YVES MILHAU AND DIDIER OBERTI
Joined Cases C-321/94, C-322/94, C-323/94 and C-324/94, 1997 ECJ CELEX LEXIS 60, [1997] ECR I-2343

Note 1 (All questions) — The Court was of the view that it needed to consider such cases based on the scope of the legislation rather than its actual enforcement. This approach has been followed in other cases (see the *French Seamen* case in Chapter 13, *infra*, for example). However, the ability of parties to invoke article 28 in a purely domestic situation as here is a significant extension of the remit of the Treaty rules. On balance however there does not seem to be another alternative since it is probably unworkable to treat a law as valid for some purposes but not others — it would be up to the French authorities to amend it so that it specifically excluded imports — and then it could be enforced.

[C] General Selling Arrangements Not Addressing Specific Products

CRIMINAL PROCEEDINGS AGAINST B. KECK AND D. MITHOUARD
Joined Cases C-267/91 and C-268/91, 1993 ECJ CELEX LEXIS 173, [1993] ECR I-6097

Note 1 (All questions) — *Keck* was a response by the ECJ to a series of references where the rules in question had only a very indirect effect on trade — see the *Torfaen BC v. B&Q. plc*, case, above.

In *Dassonville*, it will be recalled, while the product was clearly discriminated against, this was not the reason for rejecting the Belgian rule — it was the more general consequences of the rule in terms of rendering the pattern of trade different from what it might have been in the absence of the rule. In *Keck* the Court sought to restrict article 28 to rules affecting the product itself. Despite the guidance given by the ECJ in *Keck* there is certainly ambiguity as to the dividing line between rules relating to products and general trading rules. The Court has adhered to a strictly limiting doctrine. See *Centro Servizi Spediporto Srl v. Spedizioni Morittuna del Golfo*, Case C-94/ [1995] ECJ CELEX LEXIS 344, 96 [1995] ECR I-2383. *Keck* was applied in

Georgio Banchero, Case C-387/93, 1995 ECJ CELEX LEXIS 211, [1995] ECR I-4663, and *The State (Netherlands) v. Taukstation't Menkske vof and Boermans*, Joined Cases C 401-402/92 1994 ECJ CELEX LEXIS 160, [1994] ECR I-2199.

VEREINIGTE FAMILIAPRESS ZEITUNGSVERLAGS- UND VERTRIEBS GMBH v. HEINRICH BAUER VERLAG
Case C-368/95, 1997 ECJ CELEX LEXIS 316, [1997] ECR I-3689

Note 1 The Court was able to analyze the rule in question here based on its connection to newspapers rather than the more generalized sphere of games and competitions. This seemed to suit the outcome it wanted, particular as it permitted some clarification around the issue of freedom of expression (see further chapter 18, *infra*).

[D]   Rules that Reduce the Competitive Advantage of Imports

OPENBAAR MINISTERIE v. VAN TIGGELE
Case 82/77, [1978] ECR 25

Note 1 The case report indicates that the minimum price requirement was part of a scheme to introduce competition into the retail liquor business, but it does not seem to have been argued that this was a justification. The case of course preceded *Cassis*. One might therefore expect that today justificatory arguments would be made and perhaps the decision would be different. The case might be considered to have been an extrapolation of the logic in *Dassonville* which was finally brought within bounds by the *Cassis* decision and its recognition of legitimate purpose.

[E]   Rules Reflecting National Consumer Preferences or Assumptions

MINISTERE PUBLIC v. GERARD DESERBAIS
Case 286/86, 1988 ECJ CELEX LEXIS 179, [1988] ECR 4907

Note 1 First, as the materials in chapter 4 have already illustrated, the EU Treaties clearly usurp any international law relationships between the Member States. Thus the Stresa convention could not be pleaded as a pre-existing obligation. However, the principal reason for the question raised is that the convention obviously states an international standard, so France surely could not be accused of having invented its own standard as a way of protecting its national industry. Yet the Court rejected the French argument, because in its view, the product had been lawfully produced and marketed in Germany and banning its sale in France was disproportionate because labeling could have given the consumer the information that this was not "40%" fat Edam cheese. Clearly then, this type of consumer protection law is regarded as almost *per se* illegal because labeling information can provide the necessary assurance. The Court was clearly concerned about such rules which directly hinder the creation of the single market.

COMMISSION v. GERMANY
(BEER PURITY)
Case 178/84, 1987 ECJ CELEX LEXIS 20, [1987] ECR 1227

Note 1 (Both questions) — As with the Déserbais case, the priority of the single market overwhelms such arguments. But in any event such an argument is not really sustainable because Germans would still refer to foreign beers as "Bier" — what else could they call it? Presumably a label stating that the beer was brewed in accordance with the Purity Law would be sufficient for those who wanted that kind of beer. They would just have to get used to checking the label. This seems a reasonably essential precondition for securing a single market.

Chapter 7

REGULATION OF TRADES, PROFESSIONS, AND BUSINESSES

§ 7.02   GENERAL PRINCIPLES

[A]   "Regulation" by Private Organizations/The Requirement for an Economic Activity

CHRISTELLE DELIEGE v. LIGUE FRANCOPHONE DE JUDO ET DISCIPLINES ASSOCIEES ASBL, LIGUE BELGE DE JUDO ASBL, UNION EUROPEENNE DE JUDO AND FRANCOIS PACQUEE
Joined Cases C-51/96 and C-191/97, 2000 ECJ CELEX LEXIS 22, [2000] ECR I-2549

Note 1 Q1 — The guidelines offered by the Court can only be deciphered with some difficulty. The case highlights the historical requirement that individual free movement rights under the Treaty were based on pursuit of economic activity. Thus "services" not involving payment would not be covered. This was first established in the *Dona v. Mantero* case referenced in the judgment.

According to the *Dona* case, selection for an international match involving national teams might be the sole area where article 49 could not apply since obviously discrimination against non-nationals is the essence of this activity. But, even in this case, the only aspect of article 49 that would be inapplicable would be the actual non-discrimination against non-national players. It is not clear whether the Court believed that competitions between national teams would be outside the scope of article 49 even if there were aspects of such competitions that involved remuneration (such as sponsorship). References to the need for the work to be not marginal or ancillary rather obscurely suggest that this might be the case.

Certainly however, selection rules that restricted the complainant's ability to participate in commercial tournaments in other Member States would fall within article 49 if payments were made by someone to someone else in connection with an event. Television broadcasters for example would be able to charge advertisers for advertising time. Thus, in such cases, article 49 would be applicable and (as will be evident from the materials later in the chapter) it would then be necessary to evaluate the rules restricting a person's participation based on the same kind of test as first appeared in *Cassis* (see further below). In this case, the selection rules complained of were found not to be a violation of article 49.

Q2 — Article 18 states a basic right for EU citizens but does not remove the economic aspect with respect to the invocability of Treaty rights. (This is explored in depth in Chapter 16) For example, while an EU citizen has the right to reside anywhere in the EU (currently subject to further restrictions with regard to the twelve most recent entrants) the host state is still entitled to refuse entry or residence if the individual could become a burden on state resources (as, for example, in drawing unemployment benefits) unless the person can demonstrate that he or she is relying on the specific rights awarded to workers (Art 39), service providers (Art 49) or business owners (Art 43).

Note 2 The Court made plain that article 49 applies to any rules governing an activity, not just laws and other official action. This is presumably on the theory that those rules are permitted to exist under the general legal framework of the State. This certainly takes the original doctrine of direct effect discussed in chapter 2 to a level where it becomes somewhat hard to understand where the division between vertical and horizontal effect lies.

[B] Boundaries Between the Treaty Rules on Services, Goods and Establishment

STATE v. SACCHI
Case 55/73, 1974 ECJ CELEX LEXIS 47, [1974] ECR 409

Note 1 Article 31 requires that national monopolies relating to trade in goods be adjusted to avoid discrimination against out-of-state products. No similar requirement exists for services. This not to say, however, that discrimination then is permitted in the case of services. On the contrary, Article 49 may actually be more rigorous in that regard since probably it could require that a national monopoly would have to be abolished altogether. (See for example the *Höfner* case in Chapter 9, *infra*.)

Note 3 Since Article 31 has been held to be a *lex specialis* its more specific terms would override the more general prohibition on discrimination related to services in the event that elements both goods and services are involved — as in the *Sacchi* case. The practical result however could still be that the services provision would necessitate the abolition of the monopoly because of the rationale in the response to Note 1. In that regard the provisions are mutually exclusive but the more rigorous restrictions would ultimately prevail.

REINHARD GEBHARD v. CONSIGLIO DELL'ORDINE DEGLI AVVOCATI E PROCURATORI DI MILANO
Case C-55/94, [1995] ECR I-4165

Note 1 The reference in paragraph 27 does seem at odds with the *Insurance Services* case (*infra*) and also with the comments in *Van Binsbergen*. In the Insurance Services case, the Court held that the appointment of an agent in the host state was enough to bring the activities within the scope of the establishment provisions. Moreover, the Court, in the *Gebhard* case itself, refers to the principle that the services provisions are subordinate to those on establishment; and it confirms that setting up an agency constitutes an establishment given that it is quite possible to be established in two or more Member States. It seems however that the Court was anxious to emphasize that some form of temporary residence or even an office were not conclusive as to whether a person was established. It would be a question of whether that was done for a clearly temporary purpose as opposed to the conduct of a permanent business.

Note 2 What the Court means to do here is to emphasize that the question of whether someone is covered by the rules on establishment must be answered first. Only if the answer is no would one then look to the services provisions.

[C] Application of Article 43 to Non-Discriminatory Laws

JEAN REYNERS v. BELGIAN STATE
Case 2-74, [1974] ECR 631

J. KNOORS v. SECRETARY OF STATE FOR ECONOMIC AFFAIRS
Case 115/78, 1979 ECJ CELEX LEXIS 139, [1979] ECR 399

REINHARD GEBHARD v. CONSIGLIO DELL'ORDINE DEGLI AVVOCATI E PROCURATORI DI MILANO
Case C-55/94, 1995 ECJ CELEX LEXIS 443, [1995] ECR I-4165

Note 1 (All questions) — Unlike Article 49, the only element of Article 43 that could be said to be directly effective appears to be the prohibition on discrimination against non-nationals. This was the situation in *Reyners*, and the Court seemed to confirm that article 43 indeed was that narrow in scope. *Knoors* establishes that, when looked at in conjunction with Directive 64/427 the language is broad enough to cover a Member State's own nationals if they have obtained qualifications in another Member State. Thus already here, the core prohibition on discrimination against non-nationals has been broadened. By the time the Court considers *Gebhard*, it has established that the article 43 proviso regarding application of national rules in the host state must be subject to the objective justifications familiar from *Cassis*.

[D]　The Article 45 Exception

JEAN REYNERS v. BELGIAN STATE
Case 2-74, [1974] ECR 631

Note 1 The Court did not agree that the exception could be applied to an entire profession just because there might be certain aspects of the role that could be considered an exercise of official authority. Presumably then, if such particular aspects existed, a lawyer who was not a national could not perform them. However, such a person could not be barred from the entire profession for that reason.

[E]　Abuse

DIONYSIOS DIAMANTIS v. ELLINIKO DIMOSIO (GREEK STATE) AND ORGANISMOS IKONOMIKIS ANASYGKROTISIS EPICHEIRISEON AE (OAE)
Case C-373/97, 2000 ECJ CELEX LEXIS 97, [2000] ECR I-1705

Note 1 (Both questions) — The abuse provision referenced in this case is often found in civil law jurisdictions. Its application is usually confined quite narrowly and in no event could be used to prevent a shareholder exercising legitimate rights. However in other jurisdictions such as England, this concept is unknown as such. Thus one would be forced to assert only some form of EU principle regarding abuse in invocation of an EU directive. The acceptance of the legitimacy of the Greek rule must confirm that such a rule also exists at the EU level.

§ 7.03　SPECIFIC SITUATIONS

[A]　Rules Imposing a Dual Burden on Cross Border Services or Establishment — The Scope of Mutual Recognition

CRIMINAL PROCEEDINGS AGAINST ALFRED JOHN WEBB
Case 279/80, 1981 ECJ CELEX LEXIS 220 [1981] ECR 3305

Note 1 This case is an illustration of the parallel approach taken by the Court in the area of services to that in goods — effectively the application of the *Cassis* doctrine. In other words, the term "restrictions" under Article 49 does not cover any and all restrictions on services just because they might have an impact on out-of-state service providers. They will be evaluated based on their proportionality and reasonable relation to their underlying policy goal. Part of the overall evaluation of the rule would include determining whether in-state supervision is a justifiable requirement given the overall purpose of the legislation. Certainly it ought to be part of the process to examine the home-state rules to see if they provide adequate regulation. In many cases this may not however be the answer, because the home-state regulation would not apply at all to out-of-state activities and would be difficult for the home-state to police. The host state (ie here, the Netherlands) would be in a better position to regulate and could impose restrictions not only on the service provider but also on in-state service recipients in their use of such services.

THIEFFRY v. CONSEIL DE L'ORDRE DES ADVOCATS DE PARIS
Case 71/76, 1977 ECJ CELEX LEXIS 85, [1977] ECR, 765

Note 1 (Both questions) — One might start with the observation that, of all professions, the legal profession has the most justification for requiring an in-state law degree, given the need to understand the laws and procedures of the country in question. *Thieffry* does not deny the validity of this; however, if the "authorities" determine that a foreign diploma is equivalent to the national requirement, they cannot then be heard to say that the candidate, having passed the bar exam, is not qualified to practice. Such a ruling would not be justified as proportionate or reasonably related to any legitimate policy requirement.

Note 2 The Court's judgment is somewhat less unambiguous regarding this question. If the Bar Council were able to justify its failure to recognize the foreign diploma based on legitimate concerns regarding the *practice* of law, as opposed to the academic degree, it might have the right to block the candidate. Such a question was left to the national court to decide.

[B] Rules Having a Legitimate Purpose that Make Cross Border Services or Establishment More Difficult or Impossible

WOLFF & MULLER GMBH & CO. KG v. JOSE FILIPE PEREIRA FELIX
Case C-60/03, 2004 CELEX LEXIS 472, [2004] ECR I-9553

Note 1 (All questions) — The decision suggests that the Court is willing to accept requirements of this kind even if the result could be a significant reduction in the use of out-of-state service providers. The German main contractor would be exposed to liabilities that it could not recover easily because the sub-contractor is based in another country. This could therefore potentially reduce usage of contractors supplying labor from that country and even thereby have an adverse impact on that country's economy.

Note 2 The directive itself could be challenged or an action for compensation brought against the EU if it constituted an unacceptable restriction on the evaluation process, but generally speaking the Court is inclined to accept the rules as part of an overall political compromise where the EU in adopting the directive exercised a degree of discretion permitted it.

COMMISSION v. GERMANY
(LAWYERS SERVICES)
Case 427/85, 1988 ECJ CELEX LEXIS 53, [1988] ECR 1123

Note 1 Two features stand out. First, a rule applied without discrimination to domestic and foreign lawyers will be contrary to article 49 if it cannot be complied with by a foreign lawyer. That does not mean however that the rule is necessarily invalid for all purposes. It continues to apply for German lawyers. This is something of a contrast with the situation with respect to goods — see *Pistre*, chapter 6 *supra*.

Second, to the extent that the rule does place an obstacle in the way of cross border services, it is necessary to examine the purpose of the rule and determine whether it is objectively justified and proportionate to that purpose, ie the *Cassis* approach. It is particularly interesting to note that a basic test for non-discriminatory rules had already appeared in the *Van Binsbergen* case. Paradoxically, in that case, the requirement to reside within the Netherlands was a clearly prohibited restriction under the literal wording of article 49, so when the Court recognized that some residence requirements should be regarded as objectively justified it was actually introducing a modification to a rule rather than expanding a rule, as had happened in *Cassis*. Cases such as the *Alpine Investments* case appearing in Chapter 8, *infra*, confirmed that non-discriminatory rules are caught by article 49.

ORDRE DES AVOCATS AU BARREAU DE PARIS v. KLOPP
Case 107/83, 1984 ECJ CELEX LEXIS 264, [1984] ECR 2971

Note 1 The issue in this case was whether the uniform application of a national rule, putatively in compliance with the condition in Article 43, could nonetheless be invalid inasmuch as it had a specifically adverse effect on a person seeking to exercise the EU right of establishment. Thus if a lawyer wished to establish a practice in a second country in addition to his or her own, and the host country's national law prohibited establishment outside the geographical area where the practice was to be established, that rule would have a disproportionately adverse effect on the foreign attorney. In reality this was the only decision the Court could reach, because if the rule were upheld, it would seriously limit the right of establishment.

Note 2 There is no reason to suppose that Klopp would be able to do this any more than any other French avocat.

Note 4 The determination would be a question for the respective codes of conduct based on whether Klopp was acting as a German or a French attorney. To the extent that there might be overlap, as for example where the French rules purported to cover his practice in Germany, the application of such rules might be considered an unreasonable restriction and therefore a violation of Article 43.

[C] Regulation of Services Not Involving Presence in the Host State

COMMISSION v. GERMANY
(INSURANCE SERVICES)
Case 205/84, 1986 ECJ CELEX LEXIS 100, [1986] ECR 3755

Note 1 The essential dilemma presented in this case was that, if a Member State could legitimately require an out-of-state insurer to have a place of business in Germany, this would denude the service freedom of all meaning. As in *Van Binsbergen*, the Court drew a distinction between situations where the service provided in the host state was merely incidental vs. the situation where providing services to the host state constituted the principal business of the service provider. In that case the host state would be permitted to require a permanent presence in order to regulate that activity.

Note 2 Germany was still entitled to lay down rules relating to authorization to do business even in the case of purely incidental services, as long as these were not disproportionate. This clearly imposes a *Cassis* style evaluation which operates as a threshold for determining whether Article 49 applies at all. In other words, such measures would not be considered a "restriction" unless they are disproportionate.

[D] Rules Relating to the Establishment of Business Entities

THE QUEEN v. SECRETARY OF STATE FOR TRANSPORT, EX PARTE FACTORTAME LTD AND OTHERS
Case C-221/89, 1991 ECJ CELEX LEXIS 165, [1991] ECR I-3905

Note 2 No. The Court was only recognizing that the nationality of a vessel could be determined based on whether it was owned and managed within the State. If the owner was a corporation incorporated in the State, that was sufficient.

CENTROS LTD AND ERHVERVS- OG SELSKABSSTYRELSEN
Case C-212/97, 1999 ECJ CELEX LEXIS 274, [1999] ECR I-1459

Note 1 (Both questions) — The Court took a very principled view of Article 48. Since the place of incorporation is the determinant factor, and not the place of residence of its shareholders, the Corporation was entitled under the Treaty to set up a branch, and operate exclusively, in another Member State regardless of the controls in the host state designed to protect creditors and others dealing with it. The Court did not even recognize that the need to prevent fraud would justify a restriction. Although the rule was exclusively directed at foreign companies, the Court evaluated it in a similar manner to Article 28 for goods, presumably on the basis that it was part of a larger system where all companies are subject to registration in some form. The Court determined that there were other restrictive ways to deal with the policy issues than simply to prevent branch registration. Note also that the arguments made by the Danish government under Article 56 were summarily dismissed since they did not fall within any of the exceptions listed there.

ÜBERSEERING BV v. NORDIC CONSTRUCTION COMPANY BAUMANAGEMENT GMBH (NCC)
Case C-208/00, 2002 ECJ CELEX LEXIS 308, [2002] ECR I-9919

Note 1. The German rule only refused to recognize legal capacity because the central administration rule entailed that the company had to be incorporated in Germany. One can surmise that if the Dutch rule held that a company was domiciled in Germany because Dutch law was based on the location of the seat of administration, the corporation would have had to be struck from the Dutch register. In other words, the situation would not have created a problem because the corporation would have had to move its state of incorporation to Germany in order to remain a corporation.

Note 2 The reluctance is probably largely due to concerns about the ability to tax (see in that regard the *Daily Mail* case in Chapter 10, *infra*) and social concerns that had led to particular structures for corporations designed to protect workers. All of this is in flux today.

Chapter 8

REGULATION OF MARKET CONDUCT

§ 8.02 JURISDICTIONAL ASPECTS OF EU COMPETITION LAW

[A] Internal Jurisdiction — The Effect on Trade

ETABLISSEMENTS CONSTEN SARL AND GRUNDIG-VERKAUFS-GMBH v. COMMISSION
Joined Cases 56 AND 58/64 [1966] ECR 299

Note 1 (All questions) — It was evident from *Grundig* that the Court considered the "effect on trade between Member States" to be a *jurisdictional* hurdle that was easily overcome, because it did not matter here that the effect on trade might have been beneficial. It is necessary only to establish an effect, good or bad.

There is, however, a certain amount of flexibility in the concept. Generally, there seems to have been little difficulty for the Commission to establish such an effect, which may be indirect and potential. On the other hand, "subsidiarity" and "lack of EU interest" may be political reasons for declining to take action in cases where a matter is almost entirely of *intra*state concern only. From a legal standpoint, however, it is necessary in doubtful cases to engage in a rigorous analysis to ascertain whether, at the time of the practice under investigation, it was "possible to foresee with a sufficient degree of probability on the basis of a set of objective factors of law or fact that an agreement may have an influence, direct or indirect, actual or potential, on the pattern of trade between Member States such as might prejudice the aim of a single market in all the Member States." *Remia v. Commission*, Case 42/84, [1985] ECR 2545; also the *Völk* case, below.

Note 2 (All questions) — In this early case, the ECJ adopted what has been termed an "atomistic" concept of competition. That is, an arrangement that restricts *any* kind of competition, however technical, and however much it might be beneficial in a broader sphere will infringe Article 81. The purpose clearly was to establish as wide a jurisdiction for EU competition law as possible. In *Grundig* the vertical arrangement affected competition between Grundig dealers but quite possibly promoted competition among electrical appliance brands. This latter beneficial effect could be taken into account through the exemption mechanism.

VINCENZO MANFREDI v. LLOYD ADRIATICO ASSICURAZIONI SPA, ANTONIO CANNITO v. FONDIARIA SAI SPA AND NICOLO TRICARICO AND PASQUALINA MURGOLO v. ASSITALIA SPA
Joined Cases C-298/04, C-295/04 to C-298/04. 2006 ECJ CELEX LEXIS 348, [2006] ECR I-6619

Note 1 The Court emphasizes that the mere presence of foreign participants in an alleged cartel in a given Member State does not of itself establish that there is an effect on trade between Member States. The court speaks of a "sufficient degree of probability the agreement or concerted practice at issue may have an influence, direct or indirect, actual or potential, on the sale of these insurance policies . . . by operators established in other Member States and that influence is not insignificant." This kind of definition presumably could be applied by taking evidence from the foreign operators concerned but it is quite possible that they would not wish to give it. Thus the Court may not have very much factual basis for a determination. On the other hand, any evidence, however, minimal would probably justify a finding that Article 81 applied.

[B]   Appreciable Effect

FRANZ VÖLK v. ETABLISSEMENTS J. VERVAECKE
Case 5/69, [1969] ECR 295

COMMISSION NOTICE ON AGREEMENTS OF MINOR IMPORTANCE WHICH DO NOT APPRECIABLY RESTRICT COMPETITION UNDER ARTICLE 81(1) OF THE TREATY ESTABLISHING THE EUROPEAN COMMUNITY (DE MINIMIS)
[2001] OJ C 368/07I

Note 1 The ECJ speaks only of the effect on *trade*. The assessment of such appreciability calls for a case-by-case factual determination.

Note 2 By contrast with Völk, the Commission Notice above focuses only on the "appreciable effect on *competition*" and thus does not necessarily suggest that the test would be the same. In fact, the test proposed by the Commission clearly would not be easy to transpose to the effect on *trade* because it proposes analysis based on market share while holding that some provisions would be considered to have an appreciable effect on competition whatever the market share of the participants. One can note that some criteria are similar but there are differences.

STERGIOS DELIMITIS v. HENNINGER BRAU AG
Case C-234/89, 1991 ECJ CELEX LEXIS 170, [1991] ECR I-935

Note 1 The Court in the earlier De Haecht case had simply established a basic principle that it was permissible to look at a network of similar agreements to determine whether there was an appreciable effect on competition and trade between Member States. In *Delimitis*, it introduced further requirements to analyze the actual practical effects of such networks. Thus, depending on the dynamics of the market, it might be possible to conclude that the network was not a significant impediment to inter-State trade. The Court went into some depth in suggesting which factors might contribute to such a conclusion. This might include the possibility of acquisition of local breweries by out-of-state companies, the duration of the tying agreements and brand recognition. The Court also considered the effect of an access clause permitting out of state breweries to supply, at least beyond the required minimum quantities under the tying contract. This might or might not have an impact on the overall analysis depending on the reality of invoking such a clause.

Note 2 In the strict wording of Article 81, it is the agreement itself that must be anticompetitive. To require its "appreciable" effect on competition and inter-state trade to be assessed in the framework of a system of many similar agreements is to introduce an indirect causal effect. However, since the "appreciability" requirement itself is a judge-made doctrine, there seems no reason why the Court should not develop this variant of the requirement.

[C]   Extraterritorial Reach

A AHLSTROM OY AND OTHERS v. COMMISSION
Joined Cases 89/85, 104/85, 114/85, 116–117/85 and 25–129/85, 1993 ECJ CELEX LEXIS 510, [1988] ECR 5193

Note 1 (All questions) — The ECJ concluded that agreements that are directed to the EU and implemented within the EU are properly subject to EU law under international law as well as EU law. No comment needed to be made about conduct with less of a direct connection to the EU — e.g., a joint venture in the United States with products or services supplied to buyers all over the world. International law itself remains unclear about this issue.

There is clearly a practical issue of enforcement in such cases if there are no assets within the EU. However, it is clear that the Court was examining the issue from a substantive standpoint.

Note 2 The ICI case was decided on the very narrow ground that ICI (a company headquartered in the U.K., prior to the accession of the U.K. to the EC) had acted *within* the EU through its subsidiary. Thus, it is fair to say that the ICI case was not a case on extra-territorial jurisdiction at all, though this does rest on an assumption that EU competition law is permitted, by international law, to "see through" the "corporate veil" of the EU subsidiary. Moreover, the fines were levied on the parent.

The ECJ in *Wood Pulp* clearly took a more expansive approach in that it did not rely on the fact of subsidiaries or sales agents as such within the EU, but on the "implementation" of the offending agreements within the EU through sales to persons established within the EU.

Note 5 In light of the EEA case covered in Chapter 3, any agency that impinged on the autonomy of the action of the EU would be invalid. Thus the only way to proceed would be to amend the Treaty, which seems a very unlikely prospect.

[D] EU Competition Law Interaction with National Competition Laws

REGULATION 1/2003

Note 1 Paragraph 2 tries to deal with this issue. Since national authorities and national courts are now able to apply Article 81(3) as an integral part of their analysis (while under Reg. 17/62 only the Commission could grant an exemption under Article 81(3)), there is no longer the issue of what to do where the agreement is awaiting a decision for which there could be a long wait The language of Para 2 is awkward however in that it also refers to agreements "which do not restrict competition within the meaning of Article 81(1)." This could be taken to include agreements that fail to do so because of the jurisdictional test (appreciable effect), but that clearly was not the intention. Rather, the authors had in mind situations where the agreement might be considered acceptable under 81(1) because, in all the circumstances it does not restrict competition even if it does not necessarily lead to lower prices.

Note 2 The regulation does not address this issue. Rather, it continues to be a consideration in determining the size of a penalty to be imposed by the Commission or the Member State which would be judged under the proportionality test. (See further Chapter 17).

§ 8.03 EU CONSTRAINTS ON THE USE OF INTELLECTUAL PROPERTY

[A] Trademarks

CENTRAFARM BV AND ADRIAAN DE PEIJPER v. WINTHROP BV
Case 16/74, [1974] ECR 1183

[Where the owner of the same trademark in more than one Member State asserts the trademark to prevent imports from one state to the other.]

Note 1 The judgment indicates that it is the presence of national legal provisions that fail to recognize the exhaustion of trademark rights once the product has been placed on the market that is the underlying infringement of Article 28 which cannot be exempted under Article 30 since it is a flagrant restriction on trade. However, since the Court does frame the infringement in terms of the exercise of such rights by the trademark owner, one could conclude that this is an example of a situation where the

Member States are considered to be acting through their courts. It also could exemplify a situation where article 28 can be viewed as imposing obligations on individuals rather than just Member States.

Note 2 The materials later in the chapter make clear that in general the exhaustion of rights does not apply to products marketed outside the EU. This is explained by the nature of Articles 28 and 30, which solely address intra-EU trade.

Note 3 Yes, the prohibition on disguised restrictions on trade is an EU concept arising out of Article 30, and in the context of trademarks, such a restriction may be found where the trademark rights asserted go beyond the specific subject matter of such rights as defined by the Court.

VAN ZUYLEN FRERES v. HAG AG
Case 192/73 [1974] ECR 731

SA CNL-SUCAL NV v. HAG GF AG
Case C-10/89, 1990 ECJ CELEX LEXIS 364, [1990] ECR I-3711

[Where initial common ownership of the same trademark has been split up among different parties in different Member States.]

Note 1 (Both Questions) — *Van Zuylen* (No. 1) was a difficult case for the Court. It was concerned that a decision permitting the Belgian owner to prevent imports where the mark had a common origin, but there was no connection between the present owners, could lead to situations where abuses could occur — particularly where a mark was assigned to another party and then perhaps sold to someone else. However, in the meantime other cases came before the Court allowing it to develop further the exhaustion of rights doctrine to the point where it could become comfortable that situations such as that described above and in *Van Zuylen* would not constitute an abuse where there was no initial plan or capability of the original owner to use the separate national registrations to partition the market. The "common origin" doctrine, whereby the prevention of imports bearing a mark that had once been owned in both the importing and exporting states by one owner, was no longer needed.

Note 2 The exhaustion of rights doctrine also could have been used to come to the same conclusion.

BRISTOL-MYERS SQUIBB v. PARANOVA A/S AND C. H. BOEHRINGER SOHN, BOEHRINGER INGELHEIM KG AND BOEHRINGER INGELHEIM A/S v. PARANOVA A/S AND BAYER AKTIENGESELLSCHAFT AND BAYER DANMARK A/S v. PARANOVA A/S
Joined Cases C-427/93, C-429/93 and C-436/93, 1996 ECJ CELEX LEXIS 46, [1996] ECR I-3457

[Where the importer has imported and repackaged the product and applied the original trademark to the new packaging:]

Note 1 The Court engages in a rather convoluted exercise to overcome the apparent strict limitation in Article 7 of the directive that the owner cannot assert his rights unless the repackaging would adversely affect the condition of the product itself. The Court recognized that the owner's reputation could also suffer if the repackaging or relabelling were to be shoddy or inadequate in some way. As part of the cure for this, the importer would have to indicate that repackaging had occurred. But this might not be necessary if the products were being sold to users who were sufficiently knowledgeable as to the origin of the product (such as hospitals) such that they would not be influenced by the repackaging in their views of the trademark owner's reputation. At bottom, the Court is reverting to its earlier case law and concentrating on the conditions that would justify a conclusion that the owner was trying to artificially partition the market.

Note 2 Some of the comments of the Court do not seem justifiable as matters on which the Court could legitimately comment — as for example with regard to the rearrangement of blister packs so that there was no longer a batch sequence.

TERRAPIN (OVERSEAS) LTD. v. TERRANOVA INDUSTRIE C. A. KAPFERER & CO., TERRAPIN (OVERSEAS) LTD. v. TERRANOVA INDUSTRIE C. A. KAPFERER & CO.
Case 119/75, [1976] ECR 1039

[This and the next case concern importation and resale of products where the importer applies a different but similar trademark.]

Note 1 The Court draws a fundamental distinction between cases where the trademark is commonly owned, or was commonly owned at some point, and cases where one is essentially dealing with similar marks owned by entirely unconnected parties. The latter situation applied in the *Terrapin* case.

Note 2 Potentially, yes — if confusion were used as a pretext. This seems very unlikely however.

PHARMACIA & UPJOHN SA v. PARANOVA A/S
Case C-379/97, 1999 ECJ CELEX LEXIS 334, [1999] ECR I-6927

Note 1 From the Court's point of view, the issue revolves entirely around the need to prevent an artificial partitioning of the market. Thus, even if the marks in various countries were originally owned by unrelated parties their coming together under one owner would enable partitioning. Note that the Court again relies on the notion of objective necessity and proportionality — the parallel importer's rights are strictly defined by the degree to which its actions are necessary to enable it to market the product in the importing country; if it goes beyond that, then the trademark owner would be entitled to prevent it.

ZINO DAVIDOFF SA v. A & G IMPORTS LTD AND LEVI STRAUSS & CO. AND OTHERS v. TESCO STORES LTD AND OTHERS
Joined Cases C-414/99 to C-416/99, 2001 ECJ CELEX LEXIS 723, [2001] ECR I-8691

[Trademarked goods originally placed on the market in countries outside the EC/EEA.]

Note 1 The decision means to remove concerns that a trademark owner must overcome inferences that its action in marketing products outside the EC/ESA constitutes "consent." The Court does not adopt a position that consent can be inferred from silence; on the contrary it insists that the trademark owner must have positively agreed that products marketed elsewhere could be sold within the EU — the consent must be as to the placing of the goods on the market in the EU, not the absence of objection to their being imported into the EU from somewhere else.

SIRENA S.R.L. v. EDA S.R.L. AND OTHERS
Case 40/70, [1971] ECR 69

[EU Competition law Limitations on Member State trademark laws.]

Note 1 This relatively early case established the principle that intellectual property licensing and assignment generally could not be used to partition the market — the effect being to reduce competition between licensees and/or licensor across national boundaries. This therefore constitutes a different angle of attack on the same issue as arose in the Article 30 cases — the fundamental problem being the existence of national laws that enable parties to partition the market. Over the years these issues have become established to an extent that business generally understands the limitations. Moreover, the establishment of the EU trademark regulation has expressly embodied prohibitions on partitioning.

Note 2 Any argument regarding property rights (such as Article 295) will always be rendered useless to the extent that it adversely affects in any way the express freedoms in the Treaty. The property rights embodied in the ECHR would be a different matter — the EU freedoms being expressly subject to such rights, but only to the extent that the *administration* of EU law might involve specific due process issues rather than the substance of that law. (See for example the *Hauer* case covered in Chapter 4).

[B]   Patents

CENTRAFARM B.V. v. STERLING DRUG, INC.
Case 15/74, [1974] ECR 1147

Note 1 (All questions) — A patent more clearly can be seen to grant a right to be the sole manufacturer and seller of a product. Once it is on the market, however, there is no reason why the owner should continue to have protection, as long as he originally put it on the market. This could be a distinguishing feature from trademarks, which designate origin and therefore quality. In practice, however, the issue is the same — why would a trademark owner be concerned about consumer confusion where the product had in any event originated with such owner?

The purely statutory nature of patents makes a difference only insofar as some trademark rights, such as "passing off" actions, do not arise from specific statutory grants in Anglo-American systems, and indeed in code-based systems such rights exist as part of a broader set of rights as well as specifically part of a trademark legal regime. If anything, the rationality behind the application of the exhaustion of rights doctrine to patents is even more compelling.

Note 3 See *Merck v. Stephar*, Case 187/80, [1981] ECR 2063, where this situation arose and the Court ruled that such marketing exposed the patentee to parallel imports in another Member State where protection did exist. It is possible that the Court may in the future revise its views on this subject, because the result is a very harsh one and unduly impairs patentees' valuable rights. They have, after all, chosen to publish their invention to all the world in exchange for certain protections and should be entitled to defend against imports from countries where they cannot obtain such protection. On the other hand, the patentee could choose not to market the product in a state which accorded no patent protection (in this case, Italy, which did not allow the grant of patents for pharmaceuticals).

[C]   Copyright

MUSIK-VERTRIEB MEMBRAN GMBH v. GEMA
Joined Cases 55–57/80 [1981] ECR 147

Notes 1&2 The essential difference so far as copyright is concerned is that the simple *importation* of a work legitimately copied and sold in another Member State would not be an infringement of the copyright laws of the importing state unless the state *deems* its placement on the market in that state to be an infringement (as in the above case) or requires that royalties be paid in some form or to some body, thus in effect extending the protection to require payment of such royalties. This is usually a situation that most often arises where the type of work copyrighted is one where the 'copying' consists of performing it — including movies, videos, plays, musical compositions and so on. The cases have not tended therefore to deal with the simple copyright infringement issue, which probably does not have any relevance under Articles 28/30. Presumably GEMA, as protector of performers' rights would, as a result of this case, do everything it could to encourage performers not to agree to the reproduction of their works for sale in a country with a much less beneficial regime, but rather to ensure that the reproductions were first marketed in Germany where GEMA could collect higher royalties.

Note 3 *Pharmon* and *Musik-Vertrieb* do share in common the fact that an intellectual property owner permitted a third party to exploit the right and then found that it could not prevent the adverse economic consequences of that arrangement. However, in *Pharmon* the owner was allowed to enforce his rights because he had not voluntarily put the products into the market. Of course, it is also possible in copyright cases that the owner may *have* to consent to reproduction in a low-royalty country simply because of the economic and technical dominance of the recording company. All of these considerations of course seem a little dated in the era of online digital availability.

WARNER BROTHERS INC v. CHRISTIANSEN
Case 158/86, 1988 ECJ CELEX LEXIS 146, [1988] ECR 2605

Note 1 As a practical matter, the essential difference, so far as the application of Article 30 was concerned, between the *GEMA* case above and the *Warner* case is that the Danish legislation in no way operated to cause the perpetuation of price differences between the U.K. and Denmark, or otherwise to affect trade. Each state's laws relating to the payment of royalties on hiring out of videocassettes could operate without impinging on trade. The importer could be said to have sought to "abuse" the exhaustion of rights doctrine by simply buying a product in one member state and then "reproducing" it in another. This then comes close to the "specific subject-matter" of copyright, in effect the reverse situation to that pertaining in, for example, *Centrafarm*. So far as the Court's rationale was concerned, it had to respond to the argument that the owner's choice to place the video on the market in a Member State that did not grant exclusive rental rights to the owner meant that the owner lost the right to assert such rights in another Member State where it existed. The Court rejected this argument on the principle that the video rental business was essentially how owners made their money — as opposed to sales (at that time). It was clearly uncomfortable with the consequences of a different result. Furthermore one could obviously object that this would lead owners only to sell in countries that offered rental exclusivity.

Note 2 It follows from the comments on Note 1 that *reselling* the video would not legitimately give rise to a further royalty since that resale does not constitute reproduction. Renting, on the other hand, is an entirely different economic activity and takes advantage of the multiple opportunities to derive income from the same product. This constitutes a "reproduction" that has not been consented to by the author who is entitled to derive a portion of the economic benefit from this different activity.

CODITEL v. CINE VOG FILMS
Case 62/79, [1980] ECR 881

Note 1 [The "reproduction" element of videotapes as demonstrated by *Warner* is clearly evident here: "the right of copyright owner and his assigns to require fees for any showing of a film is part of the essential function of copyright in this type of literary and artistic work".]

Articles 49 and 50 were relevant here because the copyright infringement complained of was the television transmission of a movie — a service, not a transaction in goods. The argument was that the assignment of performance rights to assignees in various member states could lead to a partitioning of the market. This may indeed be so, but it is a natural consequence of the continued existence of national rather than EU rights.

Note 2 The Court follows the approach it had adopted in *Cassis* which, as was demonstrated in Chapter 6, essentially pre-empts the Article 30 exceptions. In this case, the Court recognized that the protection of intellectual property is a legitimate purpose of state legislation. Interestingly, however, it does not then follow the "reasonableness" test seen in Article 30 cases and Article 49 cases (e.g. *Van Binsbergen*) but picks up the exact language used in the Article 30 exception.

[D]   Other Forms of Intellectual Property

BELGIUM v. SPAIN
(RIOJA WINE)
Case C-388/95, 2000 ECJ CELEX LEXIS 15, [2000] ECR I-3123

Note 1 It seems that the Court was not presented with all the facts in the *Delhaize* case, leading it to the conclusion that the Spanish rule was a disguised restriction on export contrary to Article 29. In this later case it was able to conclude that there were some fundamental differences between transport within the region (among operators who knew how to handle and bottle the wine) and transport outside the region. Since it held that the rules were not contrary to Article 29, it did not reach the question whether the rules were justified under Article 30 as a protection of intellectual property. Essentially it applied the *Cassis* doctrine of evaluation here, even though it seems that the Spanish rule was principally directed to exports (but the rule did also apply to shipments in Spain itself, outside the Rioja region).

CRIMINAL PROCEEDINGS AGAINST KARL PRANTL
Case 16/83, 1984 ECJ CELEX LEXIS 214, [1984] ECR 1299

Note 1 This is rather a difficult case to rationalize. It seems that, but for the traditional use of a similar-shaped bottle in Italy, the Court might have been willing to consider the Bocksbeutel to be a designation of origin which Germany was entitled to protect through legislation. This however had "nothing to do with" the second question, which was whether the shape, having been registered as an industrial design under German law, could benefit from the exemption in Article 30. Its analysis here seems to be that since the only purpose for protecting the design was to designate origin from a particularly German region, it was not permissible and could not be justified under Article 30, again, at least where the design had already been in traditional use elsewhere. It seems almost as though the Court is passing judgment on the validity of this particular form of industrial property as being in effect unrecognized in EU law where it is used to exclude imports.

Note 2 The difference was that the Law on Designs here was not in any way directed at imports and acted therefore in the same fashion as a copyright.

[E]   The Role of the EU in Intellectual Property Protection

COUNCIL REGULATION (EC) No 40/94 [1994] OJ L11
(EU TRADEMARK)

Note 1 There was doubt that the harmonization provisions gave the EU authority to act in connection with intellectual property, particularly where it was creating, at least to some extent, a form of EU intellectual property. This will be resolved by the changes to be introduced by the Treaty of Lisbon.

Note 2 (All Questions) — The effect to the Trademark regulation is to create a sort of enforceable mutual recognition. An EU trademark is both a bundle of identical national trademarks when viewed as "property" but also has a unitary EU character. It might be somewhat paralleled in the U.S. by, say, UCC provisions that provide for filings of security interests in a uniform manner but are mutually recognized by all UCC states.

§ 8.04   OTHER FORMS OF MARKET REGULATION

ALPINE INVESTMENTS BV v. MINISTER VAN FINANCIEN
Case C-384/93, 1995 ECJ CELEX LEXIS 210, [1995] ECR I-1141

Note 1 (All questions) — The Court's analysis in this case is informative in several respects. First, Article 49 can be applicable even where the law is a purely domestic law aimed at regulating a practice that occurs on national territory. The Court did not however consider that the *Keck* doctrine applied because the restriction clearly did apply directly to services also offered across state lines. Second, the Court considered that while it would not be justifiable for a Member State to assert the protection of consumers in other Member States as a ground of justification for the measures, nonetheless, the regulating state had an interest in preserving the regulation of its own financial services industry. This case actually has a closer connection to *Keck* than the above might suggest, because it very much looks like the Court wanted to discourage the notion that a state's right to regulate services (in this area, at least) could be questioned, based on the incidental EU law aspects. Furthermore, if an argument that other Member States had no regulation could be used to undermine regulations in other Member States, the absence of EU action could cause chaotic conditions.

Chapter 9

STATE INVOLVEMENT IN ECONOMIC ACTIVITY

§ 9.02 EU POWERS: SUPPORT FOR THE AGRICULTURAL SECTOR

[A] Preemptive Effect of EU Action

PIGS MARKETING BOARD v. RAYMOND REDMOND
Case 83/78, [1978]] ECR 2347

Note 1 (Both questions) — In paragraph 65, the Court, by referencing article 29, clearly considered that the regulations amounted to a quantitative restriction on exports. One might conclude that it would have found this to be the case even if no common organization of the market had yet been created. It did however also reference the organizing regulation. The judgment seems however to focus more on the interference with the market organization and in particular pricing formation.

Note 2 Q1 — No consideration was given to the possibility that the Dutch scheme might have violated article 29, although arguably it could have. Even if it were found not to have done so, the Court would still have considered that there was a possible interference with the operation of the common organization. The approach here seems to be based on the need to analyze and if necessary obtain evidence as to whether the national scheme could in fact impede the EU common organization.

Q2/3 — The primary objection, if any, to the Dutch regulations was that the levy system could potentially encourage production of bulbs that failed to meet EU quality standards, thus requiring the national intervention fund to bear additional costs. This could have been detrimental to the EU policy regarding bulb quality. Moreover, if these costs are then funded by the levy, or thus borne by the growers, this would have an effect on the sales price and potentially exports of Dutch bulbs to other Member States, and thus distort the common market in bulbs. The Dutch government would thus have to ensure that the levies and intervention mechanisms under their scheme would not create this distorting effect, presumably by taking measures to assure that only bulbs meeting Community standards benefited from the support.

The Court's approach to preemption in these cases seems to have swung back and forth between almost an "occupy the field" view of preemption in the Milk case to opposite end of the spectrum in Van der Hulst's. Redmond lies somewhere in between. This is actually quite close to the U.S. experience. Consider for example the interplay of US and state environmental laws. The latter should not interfere with federal policy, but they can nonetheless coexist. The analysis depends on what legislative intent is manifested.

[B] Interaction with National Policies in Other Areas

R (ON THE APPLICATION OF MILK MARQUE LTD AND ANOTHER) (DAIRY INDUSTRY FEDERATION, THIRD PARTY) v. COMPETITION COMMISSION AND OTHERS
Case C-137/00, 2003 ECJ CELEX LEXIS 78, [2003] ECR I-7975

Note 1 The milk producers' arguments were based on two premises: first, that the UK's enforcement of its competition law interfered with the pricing intentions of the common organization in milk as evidenced by the intervention prices which were higher that national prevailing prices; and second, that such enforcement undermined the more general goals of the agricultural policy particularly as related to the guarantee of a fair income for producers, which had allegedly been subordinated to the interests of consumers. The Court concluded that the first argument did not preclude national measures under competition law that were aimed at the process of price formation rather than price levels themselves and that nothing in the common organization structure could be adversely affected by applying competition rules to this issue. As to the second issue, the Court clearly disliked the idea that farmers could use the agricultural policy as a justification for behaving in ways that were anticompetitive. Yet, it still required the national authorities to ensure that, in applying competition law, they did not interfere with the balance of the objectives set out in Article 33 EC. The issue was referred back to the national court for determination as to whether the application of the competition rules of the U.K. could actually interfere with the common organization's pricing mechanism as well as the more general issue of balance among the objectives of Article 33, an evaluation that the Court acknowledged required a very detailed investigation.

Note 2 As a general principle, this is correct: by adopting an approach to farm supports based on intervention in the market place, rather than production subsidies, the intent was to allow normal competitive forces to determine price levels.

§ 9.03   FINANCIAL ASSISTANCE BY THE MEMBER STATES ("STATE AIDS")

[A]   Source of Funds

COMMISSION v. FRANCE
(SOLIDARITY GRANTS)
Case 290/83, 1988 ECJ CELEX LEXIS 20, [1985] ECR 439

Note 1 The "measures equivalent" argument was used by the Commission to justify the use of the article 230 procedure. It had felt this was necessary because the French government's role was indirect — it had pressured the private fund into making the grants. This the Commission believed took it outside the scope of article 87. The Court concluded however that since Articles 87 and 89 are broad enough to cover the kind of activity at issue here, it was inappropriate for the Commission to use the article 230 procedure. Articles 87–89 provide a complete mechanism for evaluating state aids and all investigations should take place within that framework. This mechanism guarantees that all questions relative to the aid, and all parties' views, can be taken into account.

[B]   The Difference Between a Subsidy and Reimbursement for Services Rendered

ALTMARK TRANS GMBH AND
ANOTHER v. NAHVERKEHRSGESELLSCHAFT ALTMARK GMBH
Case C-280/00, 2003 ECJ CELEX LEXIS 98, [2003] ECR I-7747

Note 1 The Court draws a distinction between reimbursement for a service provided at the request of the state and financial support for a private activity conducted by the recipient. Nahverkehrsgesellschaft objected to the payments because it had been refused the concession and believed Altmark Trans needed the subsidy to survive as a company. However the Court suggested that the national court should review the criteria for a legitimate payment to determine whether in fact the reimbursement was a payment for services or a subsidy. If the winning bidder were in fact receiving a subsidy rather than simply reimbursement for uneconomic public services, this would have rendered the award illegal.

[C] Effect on Trade Between Member States

PHILIP MORRIS HOLLAND BV v. COMMISSION
Case 730/79 [1980] ECR 2671

Note 1 Q1 — The Court accepted that the Commission did not need to produce specific evidence of distortion or effect on trade. It was sufficient that the aid would strengthen the position of the recipient, thus putting it at a competitive advantage, and this would cause an alteration in the patter of trade that would otherwise have existed. Since the recipient was organized for international trade, the distortion on competition could be presumed.

Q2 — The Court did not separately analyze the effect on competition and the effect on trade. The distortion of competition would inevitably lead to the required effect on trade. This is tantamount to accepting that state aids per se distort competition and affect trade if they have any effect at all on the ability of the recipient to compete beyond national borders.

Q3 — The circumstances in which a state aid can affect trade would necessarily be different if only because the whole point of the aid is to favor a particular company, industry or region within a Member State. The distortion of inter-State trade is thus a unilateral effect rather than a direct interference in the free flow of goods or services.

Note 3 The procedures laid down in Articles 87–89 would be followed to see whether it was in the interests of the EU to allow it.

ALTMARK TRANS GMBH AND
ANOTHER v. NAHVERKEHRSGESELLSCHAFT ALTMARK GMBH
Case C-280/00, 2003 ECJ CELEX LEXIS 98, [2003] ECR I-7747

Note 1 The conclusion to be drawn from the Court's ruling is that almost any aid can be caught by Articles 87 and 88. There is no threshold in terms of the size of the undertaking, the size of the market or the value of the aid, as regards transport. The Commission, however, has applied a € 200,000 *de minimis* standard in other sectors per the Commission's notices referenced in the judgment.

[D] Relationship with Other Treaty Provisions

IANNELLI & VOLPI SPA v. DITTA PAOLO MERONI
Case 74/76, [1977] ECR 557

DUPONT DE NEMOURS ITALIANA SPA v. UNITA SANITARIA LOCALE NO 2 DI CARRARA
Case 21/88, 1990 ECJ CELEX LEXIS 100, [1990] I ECR 889

Note 1 The two cases on their face appear to take completely opposite positions. *Ianelli* holds that Articles 28/30 cannot apply to matters covered by Articles 87/88 while *DuPont* holds that, not only can they, but in fact Article 28 takes precedence. In fact, however, it is possible to reconcile the two approaches. In *Ianelli* what was complained of was the system of financing the aid — which left direct importers paying the levy but not receiving any subsidies. As it stood, this might constitute an aid to domestic industry but the system of levies was arguably valid as long as not discriminatory (the discriminatory aspects were removed after the Commission took action under article 87). Thus, the levy was indissolubly linked to the system of aid, and to apply Article 28 to it would interfere with the ability to evaluate it under Article 87. The Court specifically noted that if, on the other hand, an element of the aid system could be dissociated from the system, then it could be separately evaluated under article 28 or other articles.

In the *DuPont* case, the general system in Italy for support of the Mezzogiorno could clearly be separated from the very specific requirement for public bodies to purchase 30 % of their procurement needs from local suppliers. Applying article 28 to this requirement did not affect the overall aid system. Perhaps more importantly, the Italian rule was a direct limitation on imports, and the Court was not going to tolerate such a direct violation of the Treaty.

The Court did not attempt to reconcile the two decisions which it presumably felt did not need reconciling because they addressed different issues. This might be a little puzzling but is perhaps not atypical when dealing with constitutional provisions that are worded broadly and clearly can overlap. One might compare this with US Supreme Court interpretations — for example, whether a state rule requiring an attorney to reside in the state of admission and practice conflicts with the Commerce Clause, the Privileges and Immunities clause, or neither. It rather depends on the starting point of the analysis. It is left up to lawyers and academics to rationalize these different strands of jurisprudence.

§ 9.04   PARTICIPATION BY THE STATE IN COMMERCIAL ACTIVITY

[A]   State Monopolies

PUBBLICO MINISTERO v. MANGHERA
Case 59/75 [1976] ECR 91

Note 1 The Court had to draw on contextual interpretation. The location of this article in the section on free movement of goods allowed it to conclude that the provision was not in effect condoning import monopolies because that would clearly alter the pattern of trade. Furthermore it is understandable that a state regulation that disallows non-nationals (as well as nationals) from participating in a key element of the trade chain would be regarded as discriminating in and of itself. Note however that the removal of the monopoly on imports may not necessarily result in a liberalization of trade if there is also a monopoly on internal distribution or at the retail level. As note 3 indicates, these monopolies can continue although they may well be subject to appraisal under Articles 28 and 30.

HANSEN GMBH & CO. v. HAUPTZOLLAMT FLENSBURG
Case 91/78 [1979] ECR 935

Note 1 (All questions) — The state aid provisions and Article 31 address fundamentally different issues but can overlap where the continued existence of the monopoly as the sole purchaser of internal production is used as a means for supporting the domestic industry, as was the case here, where the excise tax was used to make up the difference between the purchase price of the domestic product and the lower selling price at retail that had come about through the abolition of the import monopoly. The court concluded that since article 31 specifically addressed monopolies, to the extent it was permitted to continue it took precedence over the state aid provisions.

[B]   Grants of Exclusive Rights to Public Undertakings or Concessionaires

[General Comment: In responding to the issues raised in the notes concerning the Article 86 cases, this more general outline may be more helpful as a prelude to answering the individual questions.]

Van Eycke (which appears further on in the chapter) represents the starting point in the analysis. The banks had not been granted special or exclusive rights (Article 86(1)), nor were they performing any of the functions described in Article 86 (2). Had they acted alone (without any involvement of the Belgian state) any agreement among them to fix interest rates could have violated Article 81(1). This, however, was not the issue in the case. Rather, the claim was that the Belgian government had, by its decree, condoned such conduct. The ECJ was very clear that because of Article 10, Member States may not carry out government policy through the medium of requiring or encouraging private enterprises to infringe EU competition rules. In the event, it seems that the Belgian decree did not condone such conduct because it laid down rules within the context of government monetary policy which each of the banks was bound to observe — compliance was in no way contingent on any agreement among the banks. However, ultimately this question was left to the national court to resolve.

Article 86(1) in one sense is nothing more than a restatement of the Article 10 principle applied specifically to the case where Member States grant special or exclusive rights to undertakings. However, the apparent significance of 86(1) is that it starts from the assumption that the actual grant of such rights is acceptable. From there one proceeds to the next question, i.e., is there anything connected with that grant, other than the special or exclusive nature of the rights themselves, that would inevitably cause the undertakings holding those rights to breach the competition rules? This issue is exemplified, with respect to Article 82, by the *Höfner and Elser* case. Following on from that is the further question of whether aspects of the grant that encourage, but do not inevitably cause, a breach of the competition rules, would also be prohibited by this paragraph. The answer ought to be no, because to the extent that the undertakings could choose whether or not to engage is in such practices, they would themselves be in violation of Articles 81 or 82 and there would be no need to proceed against the Member State itself.

The function of 86(1) then, would appear to be twofold: (a) to confirm that the grant of exclusive or special rights by Member States is not in itself a violation of the Treaty; and (b) to ensure that where undertakings are compelled, as a result of such grant, to engage in conduct that would otherwise be considered a breach by them of the competition rules, the fact that they could not then be held in breach because their conduct is not voluntary will result in a shifting of liability for the breach to the Member State in question.

Article 86(2) addresses what is in principle a completely separate situation. Its purpose is to exempt from the rules of the Treaty practices that are indispensable to the functions described there that are "entrusted" to private undertakings. Such undertakings may or may not have been granted special or exclusive rights. It does not then follow that 86(2) is intended only to be an exception to the general rule laid down in 86(1). In practice, however, it is hard to imagine an example of an undertaking that has been entrusted with the operation of a service of general economic interest that has not also been granted some form of special or exclusive right, while the concept of a revenue producing monopoly would seem inevitably to entail such a grant. From this it might be concluded that for all practical purposes 86(2) is a provision that derogates from the general principle of 86(1) by permitting anticompetitive practices where necessary for the execution of 86(2) functions.

This analysis was arguably superseded by the *Corbeau* case. Here, the ECJ held that the grant of exclusive rights by Belgium in relation to matters not directly related to a "traditional" post office's function was a violation of "article 86" by the Member State. It could be deduced from this that the grant of special or exclusive rights (or the performance of certain tasks by a state monopoly) in fact is NOT condoned by the Treaty, notwithstanding 86 (1)'s implicit acceptance of such grants, except where the purpose is to enable the carrying out of the functions listed in 86(2). The distinction between grant and abuse thus seems to have disappeared and with it, the distinct application respectively or paras (1) and (2) of Article 86.

Societe civile agricole du Centre d'insemination de la Crespelle v. Cooperative d'elevage et d'insemination artificiele du departement de la Mayenne Case C-323/93,

1994 ECJ CELEX LEXIS 401, [1993] ECR I-5077) is generally perceived to be a retreat from this extreme position in that the ECJ reverts to its concept of the inevitability of an abuse rather than the illegality of the grant of exclusivity itself. As the text indicates however, there is a distinction between *Corbeau* and *La Crespelle* in that the grant of exclusivity in the former covered an activity outside the scope of the "service of general economic interest" while in the latter the grant related directly to such service.

The text discussion of *Almelo* is correct in stating that the SEP members did not technically have exclusivity. However, they clearly had special rights that amounted to a de facto collective dominant position; but the services clearly fell within the concept of "general economic interest", so the question whether the grant of such rights might have been itself illegal simply did not arise.

HÖFNER AND ELSER v. MACROTRON GMBH
Case 41/90, 1991 ECJ CELEX LEXIS 390, [1991] ECR I-1979

Note 1 (All questions) — The grant of exclusive rights could be considered to be a violation of article 86 by the Member State where it inevitably leads to a breach of article 81 or 82 by the entity concerned. The conditions set out in the last paragraph of the judgment excerpt suggest that this was the case in *Höfner*.

Note 2 It is necessary to keep in mind here that the consequence of the ECJ's judgment — if the national court were to agree that Germany was in breach of article 86 — would be that the court would have to disregard the offending regulation. Thus the defendant company would not be able to plead the illegality of the contract, so the plaintiffs would succeed. The national court would be bound to reach that conclusion if it found that the conditions laid down by the ECJ for finding the national law to be in violation were met. Whether the court would actually so conclude would have to be a result of further investigation and evidence.

CRIMINAL PROCEEDINGS AGAINST SILVANO RASO AND OTHERS
Case C-163/96, 1998 ECJ CELEX LEXIS 281, [1998] ECR I-533

Note 1 In this case, the ECJ indicated that a State measure that placed an undertaking having exclusive rights in a position where it could not help but breach article 82 would be contrary to article 86. This seems to be a more obvious form of breach than was evident in *Höfner*. What seems to follow though from the Court's decision is that in such a case, the state is in breach of article 86 merely by granting exclusive rights. This seems to put the case in the same category as *Corbeau*.

[C]   Services of General Economic Interest

CRIMINAL PROCEEDINGS AGAINST PAUL CORBEAU
Case C-320/91, 1993 ECJ CELEX LEXIS 195, [1993] ECR I-2533

Note 1 (All questions) — This case addresses the dual situation where a grant of exclusive rights is designed also to enable the grantee to perform a service of general economic interest. As already pointed out, this is very often the case. The Court's view is that outside of the specific economic interest service (providing mail collection and delivery) the grant of exclusive rights for ancillary activities may itself be a violation of article 86 because such ancillary activities are not part of the general economic interest service. The judgment is frankly confusing and not well reasoned since it seems to overlook the right of the Member States to grant exclusive rights. It seems to conclude instead that the grant of exclusive rights for activities outside the scope of the service of general economic interest is itself a violation of article 86. The only rationale one can perhaps come up with here for this conclusion is that the extension of exclusive rights to areas of economic activity not traditionally considered to be the subject of state concession is not protected by article 86. As the general note above indicates, the Court seems to have since retreated from this extreme position.

In addition to the analysis of the Article 82 implications, the *Almelo* case is a good example of how 86(2) might apply to Article 81 situations, and in particular addresses question (c) above. Here the regional electricity distributors had received a non-exclusive concession to supply electricity in the Netherlands. Thus, a case where no exclusive rights were involved, but where there was a service of general economic interest. The producers, grouped together in an organization called SEP, had for a long time included provisions in their contracts with the regional distributors imposing exclusivity in the purchase and supply of electricity between the respective parties, thus effectively precluding any competition at that level. Such clauses would normally have infringed Article 82. However, IJM, the regional distributor defending the case, argued that they were necessitated by the conditions that would have taken away the "better" customers and left them with the uneconomic ones — whom they have to continue to supply because of their public duties. The ECJ accepted that the contractual clauses might be necessary to ensure the performance of the regional distributors' public duties and left it for the national court to make that determination.

[D]   Use of the Private Sector to Carry Out a State Policy

PASCAL VAN EYCKE v. ASPA NV
Case 267/86, 1988 ECJ CELEX LEXIS 174, [1988] ECR 4769

[The question posed here is the mirror image of that raised in the *Milk Marque* case In the *Van Eycke* decision, a national policy had the potential to impair the application of Community competition policy.]

Notes 1/2 The Court's approach here antedated Regulation 1/2003, but it is unlikely that the language of the latter would cause any re-appraisal of the Court's analysis here because of the Member States' duties under Article 10. In other words, the Court's view that Member States cannot actively further an anticompetitive practice through pursuit of other policies still holds good. In any event, Para 3 is not providing some form of exemption for Member State policies. It merely *removes* the *obligation* to apply Articles 81 or 82 to proceedings based on policies other than national competition law, and allows Member States to take action against practices which otherwise would be legitimate under 81 or 82.

Note 3 The Court was clear that its decision was based on the non-applicability of Article 81 to controls on exports outside the EU which would not appreciably affect trade between Member States. The clear implication is that if trade within the EU had been affected, the UK policy would clearly create problems.

CONSORZIO INDUSTRIE FIAMMIFERI (CIF) v. AUTORITÀ GARANTE DELLA CONCORRENZA E DEL MERCATO
Case C-198/01, 2003 ECJ CELEX LEXIS 390, [2003] ECR I-8055

Note 1 The first point to keep in mind in reading this case is that the undertakings concerned were arguing that their practices could not infringe Article 81 where they were not free to make choices on how to behave because of the state's requirements. Thus it was in their interests to argue that the state's actions necessarily resulted in anticompetitive conduct. The Court's guidance is that it is necessary to look at all aspects of competition, not just price competition (which was precluded in this case due to the Ministry's action). If the Ministry then condoned in some form restrictions on competition agreed by the private participants, this did not mean that they were free to restrict such competition. Moreover, to the extent that the Italian law might promote anticompetitive behavior it would have to be disapplied.

[E] State Investment in Private Enterprises

COMMISSION v. BELGIUM
(GOLDEN SHARE)
Case C-503/99, 2002 ECJ CELEX LEXIS 793, [2002] ECR I-4809

Note 1 The law pertaining to the golden share was very explicit about its purpose and required legally transparent and justifiable explanations by the Ministry before the rights attaching to the share could be exercised.

Note 2 The likelihood is that a justification based only on specious grounds or a desire to keep ownership within the Member State would not be upheld. As with other areas, the Court is essentially applying the *Cassis* doctrine of evaluation here to restrictions that only indirectly affect the movement of capital.

Chapter 10
STATE FINANCES AND FINANCIAL CONTROLS

§ 10.02   TAXES OR DUTIES?

INTERZUCCHERI v. DITTA REZZANO
Case 105/76 [1977] ECR 1029

COMMISSION v. DENMARK
(GROUNDNUTS)
Case 158/82 [1983] ECR 3573

Note 1 There is no exception for inspection charges for imports under EC Rules. See *Bresciani v. Amministrazione Italiana delle Fananze*, Case 87/75, [1976] ECR 129. The charge must be a part of a general internal taxation system, imposed on a non-discriminatory basis and paid for out of the public purse, or a charge for a service rendered to the importer. In the *Groundnuts* case, neither applied since the charges applied specifically to groundnuts rather than falling within a more generic system.

Note 2 (All questions) — In the *Interzuccheri* decision, the key determinant was whether the charge benefited only the domestic industry so that, even if it was levied on imports and national products alike, its differential effect on importers was sufficient to condemn it under Article 25. This would depend on the extent to which the charge on the imported goods could be considered to be considered a subsidy for the domestically produced goods, which would depend on whether it went to offset the charge incurred by the domestic industry. Thus the circumstances in which an internal fiscal charge could be considered a customs duty or equivalent are quite narrow. In the Interzuccheri case itself, the court noted that less than half the proceeds went back to the sugar industry, and it clearly was leaning in favor of treating the charge here as part of an internal taxation system, though the final fact finding was left to the national court. In the *Denmark* case by contrast, the charge was imposed by reason of crossing the frontier (between Germany and Denmark) and in that case, it must prima facie be considered a customs duty unless it could be viewed as a charge for a service rendered. To treat such a charge as part of an internal taxation system would require that it was imposed as part of a generalized taxation system applicable to all a wide variety of products for the purposes of protecting public health.

COMMISSION v. ITALY
(GAS PIPELINE TAX)
Case C-173/05, [2007] ECR NYR

Note 1 The key determinant in the Court's decision was that the tax was only chargeable if there was gas flowing through the pipeline. This was enough to render it an illegal tax on imports.

§ 10.03   INDIRECT TAXATION

[A]   Discrimination Against Imported Products

HUMBLOT v. DIRECTEUR DES SERVICES FISCAUX
Case 112/84, [1985] ECR 1367

Note 2 The ECJ did not explicitly state which paragraph of Article 90 it had in mind, but since discrimination was found, this would be considered under article 90(1), as opposed to article 90(2) which deals with comparable but different products (eg beer vs. wine). There is express discussion of the effect that the higher level of taxation had on consumers who were driven to purchase domestic vehicles because of the huge cost differential. The conclusion of the Court suggests that the tax was illegal because it fell almost totally on imported vehicles — implying that there was similarity between domestically produced and foreign vehicles.

In *Commission v. Italy*, by contrast, the tax in question operated perhaps disproportionately on some types of imported vehicles, but overall could not be discerned to favor domestic vehicles. There was therefore no discrimination. (The difference between Article 90(1) and (2) is irrelevant where there is no discrimination in any event.)

Note 3 Q1 — Of overriding importance in the *Chemial* case was the existence of an avowed national policy to discourage production of one product in favor of another, whether or not the former was produced locally or outside the territory. This, like the *Greece* case, could be viewed as a manifestation of the *Cassis* "objective justification" test in this area. The result is that no discrimination would then be found to exist.

Q2 — Clearly if an EU policy were adopted that overrode the national policy, there would no longer be an objective basis for the different treatment and the Court would then likely consider that the underlying purpose of such legislation was to protect the domestic industry. (See in this connection the *Socridis* case cited in the notes to the *John Walker* case.)

Note 4 In "domestic transactions" (i.e., within a Member State) value added tax is chargeable on the sale of goods by sellers who are registered with the relevant taxing authority. Registration is compulsory if the seller's turnover derived from the conduct of a business is in excess of a defined amount. Sales of second hand goods by private individuals not in the course of business therefore are not subject to VAT in any Member State. The price agreed by the seller for the second hand goods will, however, naturally take into account that the seller (or a previous owner) will at some point have borne VAT when purchasing the goods new.

On the other hand, at the time of the events in *Gaston Schul*, the Netherlands along with other Member States imposed VAT on all imports of goods, whether they were second hand or not and whether or not the importer was registered for VAT on domestic transactions. The importation becomes the chargeable event.

Normally in any commercial transaction in a Member State involving the export of goods, the VAT is automatically remitted to the buyer by the taxing authority of the exporting state. The importing state then imposes its rate of VAT on the invoice value of the goods, excluding the remitted VAT. In the case of second hand goods, there could be no remission of the VAT on export because the sale of the goods when new was not an export sale. Hence, as already pointed out above the price paid by the buyer in *Schul* to the seller in France, was based on a value for the goods that included the VAT originally paid on the goods by the seller when he purchased from the manufacturer or commercial supplier. Consequently, when the full rate of VAT was imposed by the Netherlands on importation, the importer essentially paid tax on a tax base that included "residual" French VAT borne by the original purchaser of the goods when new.

The ECJ ruled that the amount of Netherlands tax imposed should not exceed the amount that would have been imposed had the "residual" French tax been removed from the tax base through remission on export. For the purposes of Article 90, the discrimination arose because, if the purchase of the second hand goods had taken place in the Netherlands, the purchaser would have indirectly borne the Dutch VAT originally paid by the seller for the goods as new, while the importer had to bear not only the same Dutch VAT (directly) but also the indirect burden of the French VAT.

Private parties importing goods they have bought new in another Member State may be able to obtain remission of VAT when exporting the goods from that Member State, subject to certain thresholds and limitations. More generally, where remission is not possible, Community directives provide that they also will not have to pay VAT on importation, at least within certain limits.

[B]   Indirect Protection Between Products

JOHN WALKER AND SONS LTD v. MINISTERIUM FOR SKATTER OG AFGIFTER
Case 243/84, [1986] ECR 875

Note 1 Q1 — The Court focused on both the intrinsic properties of a product *and* the opportunities and choices to consume one or the other. At one level, the choice of the consumer may be based on factors such as taste or "image", or effect. In this case the Court concluded that the intrinsic properties rendered the products dissimilar.

Q2 — If the products fall under para (2) then, as in the John Walker case itself, there has to be an evaluation of the overall effect of the tax to determine whether it is actually providing protection to the domestic product. This requirement is not part of the analysis under para (1), where, once products are found to be similar, the test is one of discrimination.

Q3 — Not necessarily: the tax must not afford protection, but it need not necessarily be the same, in fact it very likely would not be, or if it were, this might still not be protective.

Note 2 See Note 1, Q1, above.

Note 5 Q1 — Any legislation found to infringe the free movement provisions would be invalidated. There is no scope in EU law for the kind of policy choices apparently available under the Commerce Clause.

Q3 — The Court seems to have relied on the by then fairly extensive jurisprudence in this area to conclude that cheap wine and beer could be competitive with each other. One could not make such assumptions perhaps in a new and untried area of taxation.

§ 10.04   TAXES HAVING A SPECIFIC POLICY GOAL

FRANCOIS DE COSTER v. COLLEGE DES BOURGMESTRES ET ECHEVINS DE WATERMAEL-BOITSFORT
Case C-17/00, 2001 ECJ CELEX LEXIS 293, [2001] ECR I-9445

Note 1 The ECJ alluded to the possibility that such taxes could be evaluated potentially on the basis of objective justification. However, it was not prepared to accept that a heavy handed tax was proportionate to the objective. Thus even though the tax in question was a local one designed specifically to discourage the unsightly proliferation of satellite dishes in the neighborhood, and thus arguably a wholly internal matter, its effect in this particular case was to prevent the receipt of a service from other Member States.

§ 10.05   DIRECT TAXATION

[A]   Impact of Article 39

FINANZAMT KÖLN — ALTSTADT v. ROLAND SCHUMACKER
Case C-279/93, 1995 ECJ CELEX LEXIS 186, [1995] ECR I-225

Note 1 It should be noted first that discrimination against non-residents only arises where they are essentially in the same position as residents, (the ECJ recognized that for many purposes residents were not in the same position as non-residents). These principles mean that it is unlikely that, say, Article 49 would apply, since by its terms it covers the rendering of "occasional" services and thus would not be available according to the criteria in *Schumacker*. The protection of Article 39 itself covers only cases where substantially all the non-resident's income is derived from employment in another Member State. It can be expected that further decisions will elaborate on tax issues with regard to both Article 39 and Article 45, especially since Article 45 does cover cases of persons who might be resident in one state but have set up a business in another Member State. This could apply also to corporations which may have more that one place of establishment (see Chapter 7).

Note 3 If a case similar to *Schumacker* were to come before a U.S. court, the discriminatory tax against non-residents would almost surely be struck down on the basis of either the Privileges and Immunities clause of Article IV, Section 2, or the equal protection clause of the Fourteenth Amendment, or both. In *Austin v. New Hampshire*, 420 U.S. 656 (1975), the Supreme Court struck down a state commuter income tax which was applied to the New Hampshire derived income of non-residents while exempting the income residents earned within the state. The Court held that among the "fundamental" privileges of Article IV is an "exemption from higher taxes or impositions that are paid by the other citizens of the state." 420 U.S. at 661. Also, in *Metropolitan Life Insurance Co. v. Ward*, 470 U.S. 869 (1985), the Court held that Alabama's domestic preference statute that taxed out-of-state insurance companies at a higher rate than domestic insurance companies violated the equal protection clause of the Fourteenth Amendment. Although the Court applied the rational basis test in its equal protection analysis, it found, by a 5-4 majority, that promotion of domestic business by discriminating against non-resident competitors was not a legitimate state purpose.

From a comparative perspective, it is worth noting that the factor deemed determinative by the ECJ in *Schumacker* — that substantially all the non-resident's income was derived from employment in the taxing state — would not be a significant factor in a U.S. Court.

In the U.S., as a practical matter, it is of course extremely common for a resident of one state to be employed in another. This may be resolved by an agreement between the states concerned to simplify matters by requiring the taxpayer only to file in the state of residence (as for example for Maryland residents working in the District of Columbia). A revenue sharing arrangement is then worked out. In other cases, the taxpayer will have to file multiple returns. A credit system then avoids double taxation. The issue of course is relatively less important in the US because the federal income tax is by far the more significant direct tax borne by all citizens.

[B]   Impact of Article 43

R v. H. M. TREASURY AND COMMISSIONERS OF INLAND REVENUE, EX PARTE DAILY MAIL AND GENERAL TRUST PLC
Case 81/87, 1988 ECJ CELEX LEXIS 371, [1988] ECR 5483

Note 1 It should be noted first that, unlike article 56 et seq., there is no proviso in article 43 regarding States' taxing powers. However, it is obvious that with such a strong statement in article 58 to the effect that the Member States have certain rights in this area (which effectively decouples the exception from its connection with article 56) the Member States had made clear that they did not wish the EC Treaty to affect their powers of taxation, including the detailed rules of implementation. In the *Daily Mail* case, the Court was able to find a way to protect this power by noting that the laws of the Member States have not been harmonized with respect to the domicile of corporations and thus there could be differences in the procedures that applied from a fiscal administration point of view to the removal of domicile to another State.

FUTURA PARTICIPATIONS SA AND SINGER v. ADMINISTRATION DES CONTRIBUTIONS
Case C-250/95, 1997 ECJ CELEX LEXIS 267, [1997] ECR I-2471

Note 1 Since Article 56 deals with the movement of capital it might have been thought that matters relating to the treatment of losses would be a matter falling within that area. However, one can rationalize the Court's approach by looking at the legal basis for the EC legislation — in this case the provisions on freedom of establishment.

Note 2 *Cassis* was cited because of the express reference there to the effectiveness of fiscal supervision as an overriding national interest requirement. The Court therefore engaged in a classic balancing exercise applied to indirect restrictions on a fundamental freedom.

MARKS & SPENCER PLC v. DAVID HALSEY (HER MAJESTY'S INSPECTOR OF TAXES)
Case C-446/03, 2005 ECJ CELEX LEXIS 734, [2005] ECR I-10837

Note 1 (All questions) — This case presents a detailed case-study on how the powers of the Member States in fiscal matters interact with the freedoms of establishment and services. In order to avoid distortions in the tax bases of the various states, the Court upheld restrictions on the deduction of losses from non-resident subsidiaries; but then drew the line where the risk of such distortion no longer existed — as where the non-resident subsidiary had exhausted all possibilities of deducting losses in its own state.

Note 2 (All questions) — Even in these limited circumstances, the decision here is a very significant one in that the Court did not shrink from applying the fundamental freedoms to the most closely guarded sector of state power. The UK almost certainly did not adopt the restrictions on loss deductibility as an act of comity to preserve the tax bases of other states; but no policy grounds were referenced by the Court to justify the basic principle. Neither was any consideration thought necessary as to whether parent companies could achieve their business goals through other means. The case certainly will provoke much further litigation and the ability of the Member States unilaterally to determine their definitions of the bases for taxation will be questioned. Certainly any discriminatory elements will be suspect.

[C]   Impact of Article 49

FKP SCORPIO KONZERTPRODUKTIONEN GMBH v. FINANZAMT HAMBURG-EIMSBUTTEL
Case C-290/04, 2006 ECJ CELEX LEXIS 547, [2006] ECR I-9461

Note1 It is perhaps surprising that the Court supported the German Authorities on most of the points raised in this case, given that article 49, unlike article 56 is not subject to express reservations of taxation powers. However, one could recognize that it would be difficult and perhaps politically dangerous for the Court to start laying down rules as to how tax authorities are to deal with administrative procedures relating to taxability and computation of taxable income.

[D]   Impact of Article 56

PETRI MANNINEN
Case C-319/02, 2004 ECJ CELEX LEXIS 291, [2004] ECR I-7477

Note 1 (Both Questions) — Article 56 was the basis for the analysis here because there was no question of establishment — the taxpayer was simply an investor in a company outside the state of residence, and the restrictions affected the ease or difficulty with which an individual could invest in stock of corporations outside the state of residence. Although the taxpayer was asserting the Treaty rights against his own state of nationality and residence, this was not even considered as a potential problem.

Note 2 (Both questions) — It would have been open to Finland to go in either direction to remove the source of discrimination.

Note 3 The Court drew a distinction between discrimination in the national tax law resulting from a distinctive treatment of dividends received from outside Belgium, and the uniform treatment of dividends that happened to have discriminatory effects due to the tax treatment in the state of origin of the payments (deduction at source). This seems right, given that just as in the cases concerning articles 28 or 49, the adverse treatment of the taxpayer here resulted simply from differing rules among the Member States.

HEIRS OF M. E. A. VAN HILTEN-VAN DER HEIJDEN v. INSPECTEUR VAN DE BELASTINGDIENST/PARTICULIEREN/ONDERNEMINGEN BUITENLAND TE HEERLEN
Case C-513/03, 2006 ECJ CELEX LEXIS 84, [2006] ECR I-1957

Note 1 The Court concluded that the mere transfer of residence does not come within the scope of article 56. As such, there could be no objection to a law that sought to manage the inheritance tax consequences of such a move, which did not necessarily entail the transfer of capital. This seems a rather strained interpretation, but set against the backdrop of State taxation powers, it is reasonably consistent with other decisions such as *Daily Mail*.

[E]   Articles 12 and 18

PIRKKO MARJATTA TURPEINEN
Case C-520/04, 2006 ECJ CELEX LEXIS 989, [2006] ECR I-10685

Note 1 This is the first time we encounter the rather mysterious statement of the Court that "the status of citizen of the Union is destined to be the fundamental status of nationals of the Member States." It will resurface in other other cases found in chapter 16. Essentially, the Court is acknowledging that article 18 has a certain life of its own independent of the economic freedoms. Citizens do have the right to settle anywhere in the EU as long as they are not a burden on the host state. If the state of origin then makes that right more difficult to invoke, it will violate article 18. This seems like a very fruitful area for future development of jurisprudence.

EGON SCHEMPP v. FINANZAMT MÜNCHEN
Case C-403/03, 2005 ECJ CELEX LEXIS 325, [2005] ECR I- 6421

Note 1 (All questions) — The case is chiefly interesting for the way in which the Court was able to bring the situation within the scope of EU law. The spouse's exercise of her right of free movement, though not necessarily dependent on Article 18 (she could after all have been Austrian) was sufficient to find an EU context.

Note 2 Q1/2 — The Court was clearly extremely conscious of the need to maintain the autonomy of the Member States with respect to income taxation. In fact, this seems a logical outcome in any event — the difference in the treatment of his taxation was the result of the disparity, in tax laws, as permitted by the Treaty, and not through any form of discrimination against non-residents or non-nationals.

Q3 — As an Austrian resident in Germany, he would have been subject to German tax law in the same fashion as any German national so the outcome would have been the same.

[F]   Conflicts with Other EU Policies

DE SAMVIRKENDE DANSKE LANDBOFORENINGER v. MINISTRY OF FISCAL AFFAIRS
Case 297/82 [1983] ECR 3299

Note 2 Q1 — The Danish government's policy on national incomes would have been adversely affected by the devaluation because it would have led to a sudden increase in the income of the agricultural sector due to the conversion of the intervention prices from ECUs to Danish Kroner (i.e. as a result of devaluation, the intervention prices were now translated into high Kroner prices). The tax was designed to prevent this increase by mopping up the additional income. The Court was not unequivocal about the consequences, but it would be up to the national court to determine whether the tax could have any effect on the various common organizations of the market — truly a very difficult task and hard to assess in advance.

Q2 — Perhaps there would have to be reliance on government economists or other experts as to the likely outcome. It does not seem like the ECJ expected the Danish court to gather factual evidence based on experience. The evaluation would necessarily have to be forward looking.

§ 10.06   FINANCIAL CONTROLS

[A]   Capital Controls

LUISI AND CARBONE v. MINISTERO DEL TESORO
Joined Cases 286/82 AND 26/83, 1984 ECJ CELEX LEXIS 57, [1984] ECR 377

Note 1 The very last paragraph of the above excerpt opens up the possibility that almost anyone traveling to another state can invoke EU rights. What is particularly noteworthy in this case is that the persons affected by the Italian regulations were nationals of that country. In effect therefore this case accords the Treaty rights to nationals as against their own governments. For example, if a Member State were to impose travel restrictions on students who benefit from state funded education, as for example a 3 year obligation to work in that state before taking a job in another Member State, that would potentially affect the rights of the students to receive services in other Member States and thus be contrary to Article 49. The *Müller-Fauré case*, below, deals with some of the enormous complexities opened up by this approach.

[B]   Control of State Expenditure

V.G.   MÜLLER-FAURE   AND   E.E.M.   VAN   RIET   v.   ONDERLINGE WAARBORGMAATSCHAPPIJ ZAO ZORGVERZEKERINGEN
Case C-385/99, 2003 ECJ CELEX LEXIS 739, [2003] ECR I-4509

Note 1 (All questions) — In summary, the Court went to great pains to assert the pre-eminence of Article 49 while admitting the need to balance national financial and policy considerations — thus effectively treating the application of Article 49 as an evaluation process similar to that found in the *Cassis* doctrine. The Court was clearly concerned to avoid any implication from its prior judgments (Smits & Peerbooms) that a system of prior authorization was in all cases legitimate or unconditional.

In the case of hospital care, the Court concluded that prior authorization was justified in order to preserve financial balance and access to balanced high quality healthcare. The costs of large number of people taking advantage of a system in which no prior authorization was required would upset these balances. However, the authorities need to make the prior authorization subject to objectively justified and published criteria.

In the case of non-hospital care, the Court saw no such justifications, since the numbers of people seeking General Practitioner services in another Member State was very unlikely ever to destabilize the social security system. Thus prior authorization was in principle not permissible. Instead, the Member State, as the financially responsible party for socialized medical treatment, could only require prior authorization to the extent justified by such matters as the overall financial and practical consequences of allowing patients to travel to other states.

Muller Faure also establishes that it makes no difference whether the social security system provides for benefits in kind or pecuniary reimbursement. As a practical matter this may prove difficult in some States such as the UK. The ECJ therefore acknowledged that arguments about the specific choices made in terms of the type of public health care system might justify a requirement for prior authorization even in the case of non-hospital care.

[C]   Control of Investment

MANFRED TRUMMER AND PETER MAYER
Case C-222/97, 1999 ECJ CELEX LEXIS 278, [1999] ECR I-1661

Note 1 (All questions) — The judgment is perhaps a little surprising since there could be some justifiable policy reasons for insisting that debts carrying a security interest should be in local currency. In fact, this might not be ruled out in other cases. However, in this particular instance, no justifications were put forward. It seems unlikely that the Court would take the position as far as the hypothetical question suggests since there are clearly good reasons for maintaining distinct currencies, indeed such a ruling would probably be entirely unacceptable from a political standpoint. Nonetheless, it is possible that this situation could evolve, particularly as the euro becomes more broadly used and understood outside the euro-zone.

Chapter 11
EXTERNAL RELATIONS

§ 11.02   LEGAL BASIS

OPINION 2/00
(CARTAGENA PROTOCOL)
2001 ECJ CELEX LEXIS 364, [2001] ECR I-9713

PARLIAMENT v. COUNCIL AND COMMISSION
(PASSENGER NAME RECORDS/"PNR")
Joined cases C-317/04 and C-318/04, 2006 ECJ CELEX LEXIS 926, [2006] ECR I-4721

Note 1 Q1 — In the first place, as will have become clear by now, there are no EU inherent competences. In the U.S. the general power to enter into Treaties enjoyed by the United States (as opposed to the various States) derives from the Constitution. As noted in the introduction to this chapter, it is also noteworthy that the original 13 colonies never existed as independent states as subjects of international law in the same way that the EU Member States did and still do. The EU has only conferred powers, and thus it is always necessary to find a legal source for action, be it internal or external. The identification of the specific source is important because it defines both the extent of the power and whether it is exclusive. It also defines the procedure to be followed internally, and in particular whether the Parliament should be involved.

Q2 — If indeed the EU had no power to enter into a particular treaty, then the Member States would need to do so. They could also act through the European Council under the CFSP to delegate such power to the Council.

§ 11.03   THE BASES FOR EXCLUSIVE COMPETENCE UNDER THE EC TREATY

[A]   Article 133 — The Common Commercial Policy

OPINION 1/75
(LOCAL COST STANDARD)
[1975] ECR 1355

Note 1 Q1 — The exclusivity of the common commercial policy derives from the need to ensure the "defense" of the common interests of the EU. In this particular case, unilateral action by Member States in the area of export credits would lead to distortion of competition among EU firms in third country export markets. This need for uniformity takes precedence over the powers retained by the states to finance systems of export credits.

Q2 — The opening remarks make it clear that the common commercial policy has an external *and* an internal component. Thus, the situation discussed in the introduction to this chapter as regards the United States does not arise within the EU; the common commercial policy has preemptive effect as an internal policy and does not then grant powers externally for which there is no express internal grant. It must, nonetheless, be recognized that, pursuant to the common policy, the EU may enter into agreements that preempt national laws. In this case, the EU had already acted to harmonize the basis for determining export insurance.

OPINION 1/78
(INTERNATIONAL AGREEMENT ON NATURAL RUBBER)
[1979] ECR 2871

Note 1(Both questions) — The Court first concluded that the overlapping of general economic policy (reserved to the Member States) and commercial policy (reserved to the EU) could not be a ground for denying the powers of the EU to conclude this agreement. The Court then examined the implications of the financing arrangements for the buffer stocks. One alternative was that these arrangements would be assured out of Member State public finances. Nonetheless, they were only a component of the overall agreement that fell under the commercial policy. If the Council were to decide that the financing were to be left to the Member States, then they would have to be involved in the decision making machinery aimed at intervention in the world market.

The Court seemed very clear that there was no automatic right for the Member States to participate. Thus, it could be argued, this was not a genuine case of shared competences, but only implementation; the commitments under the agreement itself could involve requirements for the states *in principle* to make funding available, but they would have a say in how much, when and for what such funding should be made. On the other hand, the Court also indicated that a decision to fund by Member State contributions would take that element *out* of the *exclusive* competence of the EU.

Note 2 (All questions) — Given the exclusive powers of the EU under Article 133, the powers of the Member States and the EU would have to be several rather than joint. The EU ought not to be responsible for failures by the Member States within their sphere of competence. If the distinction between their responsibilities is not clearly laid down in the agreement in question, there is a danger that the EU could be held liable for Member States' breaches and vice versa under general principles of international treaty law.

OPINION 1/94
(AGREEMENT ESTABLISHING THE WORLD TRADE ORGANISATION)
1994 ECJ CELEX LEXIS 459, [1994] ECR I-5627

Notes 1 Q1 — The Court had no difficulty establishing a general exclusive competence for the EU relating to goods. With services, however, the difficulty arises where the agreements in question envisage liberalization of controls on the free movement of persons. Under the EC Treaty, these are referred to specifically and separately from commercial matters and therefore would not be considered to fall under Article 133.

In relation to intellectual property, the EU has exclusive competence regarding measures to prevent trade in counterfeit goods, but beyond this the Member States remain competent.

Q2 — The above considerations referenced the structure of the EC Treaty as a means of delineating the scope of article 133, but this does not mean that its scope is actually dependent on internal powers.

Note 2 (Both questions) — The Court was able to limit Article 37 to internal competence even though a directive purporting to deal with external matters had been validly adopted under it. In the ECJ's view, the directive was designed to give *internal* effect to an external arrangement. The clear intention was to treat all external commercial matters as falling under Article 33, which makes sense because, unlike the provisions on agriculture, there are express mechanisms to ensure that agreements are negotiated, ratified and executed in accordance with a "constitutional" procedure.

[B]   Other Bases for Exclusive Competences

COMMISSION v. COUNCIL
(ERTA/AETR)
Case 22/70, [1971] ECR 263

Note 1 It is evident that the issue is not one of internal powers, but rather, whether external action would interfere with an internal EU policy.

Note 2 The Court clearly took the view that Article 133 was intended to cover "tariff and trade agreements". Since article 133 is also an internal policy, it was necessary to define the boundaries between it and other policies such as transport. This logic seems somewhat at odds with the reasoning the WTO where article 37 was used as the basis for implementing internally some external action, but this did not prevent the application of article 133 in that area.

Note 3 This question concerns the CFSP. As seen in Chapter 5, there is the possibility of "creeping" federalization through the gradual transfer of powers to the Council, at least to implement policies, if not to make policy. It should be remembered that although the ECJ does not have jurisdiction over CFSP as such, it can be involved in defining how this might then affect the relative competences under the EC Treaty (see chapter 5).

Note 4 The Article 300 procedure applies, even though the Treaty doe not expressly say so.

OFFICIER VAN JUSTITIE v. CORNELIS KRAMER AND OTHERS
Joined Cases 3, 4 and 6/76 [1976] ECR 1279

Note 1 Some commentators had drawn conclusions of a more general nature from *Kramer*, suggesting that indeed preemption in external matters meant "occupying the field", thus precluding all state powers in an area even if the EU had not at the time acted. However, it seems clear from the EC Treaty and the U.K./Ireland/Denmark Act of Accession that the EU had *decided* to proceed by common action within the Fisheries Commission, so there had been an "express" grant of powers to the EU, bringing foreign policy within this area into the same category as the Article 133 commercial policy. The case is thus quite fact specific.

Note 2 It is certainly not unknown for other signatory states to object to the participation of the EU in an international organization or convention. Where the EU is unable to overcome the objections, the Member States may have to continue to participate, but from an EU law perspective, they do so purely as representatives of the EU.

OPINION 1/76
(LAYING UP FUND)
[1977] ECR 741

Note 1. Here there was no dispute that the EU had the power to enter into an agreement with Switzerland. Rather, the Court expressed a principle that if an internal policy *required* external agreement to be effective, then only the EU had the power to enter into it.

Note 2 (Both questions) — Some of the EU Member States had to participate because they were parties to a convention covering the subject matter of the agreement. They were therefore participating as necessary "third parties", while the agreement was binding on the EU by reason of the EU's own act. Member States were not entitled to participate in the negotiations in usurpation of EU powers. The problem that transpired is not dissimilar to the issues confronted by the Court in the EEC cases (Chapter 3 *supra.*) The Member States had overstepped the bounds of what they could do within the organization.

Note 3 Yes, and this is indeed what now happens (and is endorsed in the Lisbon Treaty).

OPINION 1/94,
(AGREEMENT ESTABLISHING THE WORLD TRADE ORGANIZATION)
1994 ECJ CELEX LEXIS 459, [1994] ECR I-5627

Note 1 The language does confirm this but the language in *ERTA* was thought by some commentators to herald a broader approach than eventually transpired per the *WTO Opinion.*

Note 2 In *WTO* the Court stresses that for *1/76* to apply it is necessary to examine whether the internal rules required an international agreement to be effective. This was not the case, it found, with respect to GATS, since the EU rules could and did exist independently of GATS.

Note 3 (All questions) — This is a clear example of the point made in the introduction in Chapter 5. Harmonization is achieved through legally binding acts which represent policy choices by the EU. Hence, from then on, the Member States cannot take action that would interfere with the unfettered functioning of such policy.

Note 4 The Court dismisses entirely the notion that Article 308 could act to confer external competences on the EU by itself. Clearly the Court's view is that this article is simply a mechanical device to ensure that objectives of the Treaty in areas of established EU competences can be attained.

COMMISSION v. BELGIUM
(OPEN SKIES)
Case C-471/98, 2002 ECJ CELEX LEXIS 37, [2002] ECR I-9681

Note 1 The principles are as follows:

(1) Look first to see whether the subject matter falls within a specific area of external relations competence such as article 133

(2) Does the subject matter require an international agreement in order to be effective within the EU? In that case the EU has the exclusive authority even if it has not acted internally.

(3) If internal rules, however broad, have been adopted, then any action internationally by a Member State is outside its competence even if the action it takes does not actually interfere with the internal rules — it is sufficient that it could, or put another way, that it overlaps in some way with the internal rules.

Note 3 (Both questions) — Obviously the ruling here involves a great degree of legal complexity. This imposes a considerable duty on the Member State to ensure it actually has the powers to act in the international field. Inevitably, this pushes competence further in the direction of the EU.

§ 11.04 MIXED AGREEMENTS

OPINION 1/94
(WTO AGREEMENT)
1994 ECJ CELEX LEXIS 459, [1994] ECR I-5627

Note 1 The Court stated, in response to the concerns about how mixed agreements could create enormous problems and endless bickering about competence, that the Member States had a duty of co-operation: "That obligation to cooperate flows from the requirement of unity in the international representation of the Community." Presumably this would flow from their duty of sincere co-operation under article 10.

COMMISSION v. IRELAND
(NUCLEAR REPROCESSING)
Case C-459/03, 2006 ECJ CELEX LEXIS 238, [2006] ECR I-4635

Note 1 (Both questions) — Given the reference to article 10 EC, it may be assumed that very little of what still lies within the competence of the Member States can be treated as having no EU connection at all; thus they must at the very least consult with the EU before taking any significant international action. As a practical matter this already happens and indeed is built into the CFSP pillar. This case however suggests that they will be in breach of the EC Treaty in many instances, whether or not there has been co-ordination under CFSP.

§ 11.05 SURRENDER OF POWERS FROM THE EU TO THE MEMBER STATES OR TO OTHER BODIES

BULK OIL (ZUG) AG v. SUN INTERNATIONAL LTD AND SUN OIL TRADING CO
Case 174/84, 1986 ECJ CELEX LEXIS 95, [1986] ECR 559

Note 1 (All questions) — The Court seems to treat the activity of the Member State here as within a legitimate and express exclusion by the Council of oil products, given, in particular, the special commitments undertaken by some Member States to third states. If this were to lead to contradiction of EU policies, presumably the Council could step in and control the activities. The issue is fundamentally different from that in *WTO* and *Laying Up Fund* because here the matter does remain fully under EU control.

Note 2 The situation is, again, fundamentally different from that of directives. There was no question that the common commercial policy had become exclusively an EU matter, and the Member States could only act by derogation granted by the EU.

Note 3 (Both questions) — The Council's exercise of its discretion in this regard is based on a pragmatic approach that allowed certain policies to remain in place that satisfied overall EU objectives at least on a provisional basis.

§ 11.06 COMPETENCE AS BETWEEN THE TEU AND THE EC TREATY

AHMED ALI YUSUF AND AL BARAKAAT INTERNATIONAL FOUNDATION v. COUNCIL AND COMMISSION
Case T-306/01, 2005 ECJ CELEX LEXIS 422, [2005] ECR II 3533

Note 1 Q1 — The jurisdiction could be considered dependent on whether the issue addressed involved another sovereign state or an analogous situation.

Q2 — Overall the Commission's position seems to challenge one's instinct that regulations of this kind really belong under the CFSP rather than the economic sphere of the EC Treaty, and the Court declined to accept the arguments based on article 308, underpinned by articles 60 and 301.

Part IV
EU GOVERNANCE

Chapter 12

LEGISLATIVE AND RULEMAKING PROCESSES

§ 12.02 "PRIMARY" LEGISLATION

[A] Is There a Legislature?

MATTHEWS v. UNITED KINGDOM
(App. no. 24833/94), EUROPEAN COURT OF HUMAN RIGHTS,
(1998) 28 EHRR 361, [1999] ECHR 24833/94

Note 1 Q1 — The Court first reviewed the case-law of the ECHR to determine whether the protocol in question was broad enough to cover bodies of an organization that is not itself a state or a party to the Convention. Having concluded that it was, the Court then took into account the special characteristics of the EC as a supranational body in order to make any allowances that might require. It then looked at the functions actually performed by the Parliament, and determined that it had moved far enough away from a consultative role to a role of active participation in the formation of legislation to be considered as a legislature.

Q2 — The absence of the right to initiate legislation is a significant gap, and could justify the argument, but it is all rather subjective and dependent upon definitions at a time when state and international law institutions are evolving, which might require us to rethink those definitions.

Note 2 While the Council undoubtedly represents the Member States, it does not fit the model in several respects: its composition varies depending on the subject matter; it works closely with the Member States through COREPER; it is not elected as an EU body; it has virtually no power of initiative (like the Parliament); and it takes political direction from the European Council.

Note 3 Q1 — The original concept underlying this requirement is that the Commission is the "guardian" of the Treaties and is the only party that could be trusted to come up with proposals that would be in the EU interest. If Member States could initiate such proposals, this would likely have been very divisive.

Q2 — As to the difference between proposals and recommendations, the legal procedures applicable to actions and voting on proposals from the Commission mean that depending on the subject matter, turning down a proposal may require a certain minimum number of votes. Proposals also require action within deadlines.

Q3 — Of course there is nothing unusual about the executive's making proposals for legislation in any democracy, but a rigid separation of powers is unusual outside the US so the executive role is really built into the legislature because the governing party serves in both roles (parliamentary democracy).

Q4 — The essential difference is that under Article 251 a proposal ultimately dies if not approved by the Council and the Parliament,

Note 6 Q1 — The general consensus is that the Luxembourg Accords have no legal foundation. If such a situation as gave rise to them were to occur again, it is unlikely they would be invoked. The voting structure has undergone so much evolution and is now so finely balanced that the pressure on any Member State to go along with the rules would likely be sufficient to avert a crisis. Moreover, it is always open to any Member State to seek redress in the ECJ.

Q2 — The decision is legally binding but it is hard to discern any meaning in it.

PARLIAMENT v. COUNCIL AND COMMISSION
(AID TO BANGLADESH)
Joined Cases 181/91 and 248/91, 1993 ECJ CELEX LEXIS 139, [1993] ECR I-3685

Note 1 The ECJ did not consider that acts of the Member States were part of EU law, hence its conclusion that it had no jurisdiction. It would be different however if the Member States had taken such a decision when the power had become vested in the EC. That would open the way for an Article 226 action.

The decision merely reinforces the notion that the Treaties, while containing some Constitutional type provisions, do not in any way serve as an overall umbrella for the structure of the EU and its constituent Member States. Admittedly the TEU clearly has more of a constitutional scope, but even here it is not a "federal" constitution seeking to regulate all aspects of the federal "state". The Constitution Treaty language would have effected some significant changes in this regard, while the Reform Treaty binds the EC and EU Treaties into a single Union with only the EU surviving as successor to the Communities.

It is surely a prominent feature of the unique EU/EC lawmaking process that an act which to all outward appearances looks like an EU legislative act should be held not to have that quality. This reflects the dual status of the representatives of the Member States as delegates to the Council and as representatives in an international conference. Such acts would be very unusual today because they would likely be caught in the framework of the EU, with the Council acting as the body of that organization rather than the Commission. This however only underscores again the unique nature of the processes.

Note 2 The involvement of the Commission is perhaps the most confusing part of this decision. The Commission after all is *only* an EU body, yet apparently the Member States were able to confer a mandate on it outside the scope of the EU. The Court tells us that one should have regard to the content of the act and all the circumstances surrounding its adoption. The key determinant here was that the act relied on funding by the Member States and not by the EU. At the time, the Parliament could only bring actions under article 230 in order to protect its prerogatives. In this case they were not infringed because no EU expenditure was involved, thus the action was inadmissible.

[B]   Procedural Requirements

PARLIAMENT v. COUNCIL
(TRANSPORT INFRASTRUCTURE COSTS)
Case C-21/94, 1995 ECJ CELEX LEXIS 430, [1995] ECR I-1827

Note 1 The key issue was the significant change in the proposal. Clearly it would be unacceptable for the Council to consult on a proposal from the Commission and then act on a revision which was no longer reflective of the first in some material way. Here the significant change had been that a requirement for the Commission to submit proposals had been changed to an option ("if necessary").

Note 2 Q1 — The Court was concerned to avoid legal uncertainty.

Q2 — Only insofar as it preserved the status quo. The need to re-adopt could lead to changes for the future but this would be true of any legislation.

Q3 — This was not a waste of time because the Parliament might actually suggest changes that would be accepted.

SA ROQUETTE FRERES v. COUNCIL
Case 138/79, [1980] ECR 3333

Note 1 This seems extremely unlikely. The Parliament's participation in co-decision is growing and it would likely not want to give any encouragement to expand the use of the consultation procedure which does not give it the last word on legislation.

PARLIAMENT v. COUNCIL
(DEVELOPMENT FINANCE REGULATION)
Case 316/91, 1994 ECJ CELEX LEXIS 24, [1994] ECR I-625

Note 1 The concern here was that the Council had sought to circumvent the Parliament's right to be consulted under the financial regulation provisions rather than on an optional basis, which is what had happened. The Council was concerned to preserve its prerogative in this regard.

[C] The Requirement to State Reasons and the Legal Basis for Legislation

COMMISSION v. COUNCIL
(TEXTILE PRODUCTS)
Case 45/86, [1987] ECR 1493

Note 1 (All questions) — The central point of this decision is that the Council had not specified the legal basis for its action. The preamble should have done this but did not, and it was impossible to discern clearly what was intended as a legal basis from the context and content. This was important particularly here because a choice of legal basis could make a difference to the legislative process. Interestingly, this might be the sort of case that could have been averted if the proposal for the TEU mentioned in Chapter 5 for a reference procedure to the Court on subsidiarity (assuming it would encompass other grounds as well) had been accepted. However, as discussed in Chapter 5 this was not a feasible idea. The Court sought to determine what would have been the correct legal basis by looking at the scope of Article 133. Since as seen in Chapter 5, Article 308 cannot be used where another Treaty provision is available, this was an easier exercise than that which it had to undertake in the next case.

Note 2 It is conceivable but unlikely that major conflicts would occur due to the continuity and unity of the Council's secretariat.

THE QUEEN v. SECRETARY OF STATE FOR HEALTH, EX PARTE BRITISH AMERICAN TOBACCO (INVESTMENTS) LTD AND IMPERIAL TOBACCO LTD.
Case C-491/01, 2002 ECJ CELEX LEXIS 628, [2002] ECR I-11453

Note 1 Since the use of more than one legislative base would give rise to conflicts as to the type of procedure to be followed, the Court has indicated that if there is a predominant basis, this should be used solely. The conclusion from the Court's reasoning, where as here, a second basis was improperly relied on is that the difference in voting requirements between the two bases would compromise the measure, but if in both instances a qualified majority is required "no harm is done."

[D] Advice and Consent

PARLIAMENT v. COUNCIL
(MAURITANIA)
Case C-189/97, 1999 ECJ CELEX LEXIS 267, [1999] ECR I-4741

Note 1 Q1 — The case highlights what is likely to be an increasing issue as the legislation of the EU expands. The Court is then called to arbitrate over what were in their origin essentially political devices and so the results from a legal point of view will never be very satisfactory.

Q2 — Yes. The Court looked at the reality within the context of the external relations budget which seems to be what the article intended.

Note 2 Q1 — This is a valid argument but in reverse. Decisions by Member States around international obligations would normally be expected to follow a ratification procedure. To allow an argument like this to prevail based on an internal appropriation issue might well be surprising. Thus the Court was right to dismiss the Parliament's argument.

Q2/3 — Arguably not: the fault, if there is one, lies with article 300 as a whole, which requires only consultation. The EU system creates a hybrid where the Council both "ratifies" by approving a decision or regulation authorizing signature, and signs the agreement (via whomever is serving as President). Of course, in any state where an international agreement requires substantial changes or increases in funding, there must be agreement by all the organs of government that have the ability to block such funding, or the State will find itself in breach of its international obligations. Thus it does actually seem appropriate to have included the Parliament in this process for that reason.

§ 12.03 IMPLEMENTING LEGISLATION OR "RULEMAKING"

[A] Division of Responsibilities Between Institutions

FRANCE, ITALY, AND UNITED KINGDOM v. COMMISSION (TRANSPARENCY DIRECTIVE)
Joined Cases 188 and 190/80, [1982] ECR 2545

Note 1 (Both questions) — The directive is seen as an instrument of primary legislation, a role reserved to the Council and Parliament. However, the definition of a directive does not preclude its use as an implementing measure. Moreover Article 86 does not specifically authorize the use of directives by the Commission. The Member States however objected to the general nature of the directive, arguing instead that, since the Commission has only implementing powers its directives should be analogized to individual decisions. Fundamentally then, this was an issue regarding the division of powers. The only argument that the Court took seriously was that the Council's powers under Article 89 trumped the Commission's powers under Article 86(3). The Court rejected the argument based on analysis of the provisions themselves and pointing out that the 86(3) power was at a different stage, preliminary to the actions that might be taken under Articles 87 and 88.

Note 2 In fact the nature of the directive in issue here was quite different from the kind of act adopted by the Council in a legislative context. It was much closer to a decision in that it simply required the Member States to take executive action, not adopt legislation. There is actually nothing in the nature of a directive to suggest that it must require intervening legislative action.

COMMISSION v. COUNCIL (CCI ANNEXES)
Case C-257/01, 2005 ECJ CELEX LEXIS 31, [2005] ECR I-345

Note 1 Q1 — As indicated by Article 202 EC, the Council can reserve implementing measures to itself for specific purposes provided it gives valid reasons. The visas judgment is explicit in recognizing the inherent balance between the institutions as evidenced by Article 202, which is why specific reasons must be given.

Q2 — This was relevant insofar as the whole area was in a state of transition, so it made sense to reserve this to the Member States until other aspects had been finalized.

[B] Involvement of the Member States in the Rulemaking Process — Consultation or Delegation?

COUNCIL DECISION 1999/468 EC
1999 OJ L 184

EINFUHR- UND VORRATSSTELLE FÜR GETREIDE UND FUTTERMITTEL v. KOESTER, BERODT & CO.
2Case 5/70, [1970] ECR 1161

Note 1 The Court drew a distinction between committees with advisory powers (even if the Commission has to defer a decision or consult the Council) and an actual participation in the decision. Thus there had been no wrongful delegation of powers.

COMMISSION v. PARLIAMENT AND COUNCIL
(FINANCIAL INSTRUMENT FOR THE ENVIRONMENT — LIFE)
Case C-378/00, 2003 ECJ CELEX LEXIS 118, [2003] ECR I-937

Note 1 The Court did not consider the non-binding character of the second Comitology decision to be sufficient to permit the Council to digress from it without giving legally acceptable reasons. In effect, this case turns on an inadequacy of the reasons given in the Regulation, the Court viewed the failure to explain why the Comitology decision rationales were not followed to be a failure to give adequate reasons for that aspect of the legislation, which then caused entire regulation to fail.

[C] EU Rulemaking by the Member States?

COMMISSION v. COUNCIL
(CCI ANNEXES)
Case C-257/01, 2005 ECJ CELEX LEXIS 31, [2005] ECR I-345

Note 1 The Court considered that in this particular case, the Member States had previously had competence to administer aspects of the Schengen Convention and thus to make changes themselves, and the incorporation of the Schengen rules into the EC Treaty did not deprive them of that ability unless it could be shown that the failure to adopt uniform rules could jeopardize the implementation of the rules once they became part of EU law.

§ 12.04 PUBLIC ACCESS

REGULATION (EC) NO 1049/2001 OF THE EUROPEAN PARLIAMENT AND OF THE COUNCIL
[2001] OJ L 145

MAURIZIO TURCO v. COUNCIL
Case T-84/03, 2004 ECJ CELEX LEXIS 568, [2004] ECR II-4061

Note 2 The Council was relying on an exception which had to be interpreted strictly. It thus was required to consider the content of the opinion in determining to withhold; but it did not have to divulge any of the opinion once it could show that it had considered this issue.

IFAW INTERNATIONALER TIERSCHUTZ-FONDS GGMBH v. COMMISSION
Case T-168/02, 2004 ECJ CELEX LEXIS 573, [2004] ECR II-4135

Note 1 The regulation only deals with documents in the possession of the EU institutions. If a Member State would not be required to divulge a document under national law, it would clearly be reluctant to give it to the EU institutions unless it had an absolute right to refuse permission to hand it over to a private individual. Thus, far from depriving the access rules of effectiveness, this rule actually facilitates transparency, since, except where the Member State objects, documents may be made public at the EU level which they would not have been at the state level.

Chapter 13

THE EU EXECUTIVE

§ 13.02   GENERAL PRINCIPLES REGARDING EXECUTIVE ACTION

[A]   Authorization

UNITED KINGDOM v. COMMISSION
(SOCIAL EXCLUSION PROGRAM)
Case C-106/96, 1998 CELEX LEXIS, [1998] ECR I-2729

Note 1 The UK had asserted what is a fairly standard authorization requirement in any business or public administration, that approval of a budget does not mean approval for individual expenditures without a separate decision (usually above a certain amount).

Note 2 The case does suggest that, if the requirement for authorizations for individual items is set too low, the Commission would find itself unable to carry out essential tasks. However, there is no evidence that this has been a concern.

[B]   Delegation of Discretionary Powers

MERONI & CO., INDUSTRIE METALLURGICHE, S.A.S. v. HIGH AUTHORITY OF THE EUROPEAN COAL AND STEEL COMMUNITY
Case 10/56, [1957 & 1958] ECR 157

Note 2 Q1/2/3 — The delegation was invalidated because a measure of discretion was granted to the independent "Brussels agencies." This delegation deprived the undertakings regulated by the ECSC of their guarantees and protections under the Treaty. Although the Court was not specific as to what these were, it obviously had in mind:

- The duty to state reasons for the body's decision and to refer to any opinions required to be obtained;
- The duty to publish annually a general report on the body's activities and administrative expenses;
- The duty to publish data useful to governments and others;
- The possibility of judicial review.

Q4 —. Today such delegations, under the EC Treaty, would still not be acceptable because the protection of persons affected by such actions must be assured through the right of challenge to acts of the "institutions" under Article 230 EC (where a delegation is legal — involving no discretion — the act of the body in question would be considered the act of the Community — see the *Akzo* case below).

AKZO CHEMIE BV AND AKZO CHEMIE UK LTD v. COMMISSION
Case 5/85, 1986 ECJ CELEX LEXIS 257, [1986] ECR 2585

Note 1 Q1/2 — Given the European role assigned to the Commission, the notion that collegiate decisions were necessary to ensure each Member State's representation is clearly antithetical to the very reason for the Commission's existence. In any event, these proceedings involve companies, not States.

Q3 — The delegation was acceptable since it was necessary for the efficient operation of the administration. Even though some discretion was involved, the rights of the undertakings were not impaired since they could treat the act as one of the Commission itself (unlike in *Meroni*).

FIRMA WILHELM FROMME v.
BUNDESANSTALT FÜR LANDWIRTSCHAFTLICHE MARKTORDNUNG
Case 54/81, [1982] ECR 1449

Note 1 Q1 — The ECJ expressly recognized that there may be divergences in treatment as between Member States, but has at least tried to lay down some minimum standards to ensure the accomplishment of Community objectives: see e.g., *Balkan Import-Export GmbH* v. *Hauptzollamt Berlin-Packhof*, Case 118/76, [1977] ECR 1177. The limitations are clearly spelled out in *Fromme* — based on assuring equivalence to national protection.

Q2 — The national authorities are not regarded as EU institutions, nor, technically is there a "delegation". Today they are described as "agents" of the EU. However, the Commission could in theory take over the functions carved out by the Member States. See also: *Nold v. High Authority*, Case 18/57, [1959] ECR 121; *Alliance Nationale des Mutualités Chrétiennes and Institut National d'Assurance Maladie Invalidité* v. *Rzepa*, Case 35/74, [1974] ECR 1241.

Note 4 The Commission's role here would probably be acceptable as long as it did not involve any action that would give rise directly to legal consequences.

[C]   Independence

FRANCE v. COMMISSION
(COOPERATION AGREEMENT)
Case C-233/02, 2004 ECJ CELEX LEXIS 151, [2004] ECR I-2759

Note 1 (All questions) — It is important to draw a distinction between the role of the Commission and the role of the EU. The Commission may be given executive powers to regulate specific agreements with other countries on behalf of the EU which can then be rendered part of EU law by action of the Council and the Parliament. But the Commission has no implied power to enter into any form of agreement *qua* Commission that would hinder its freedom of action. Thus, the Court could only condone the guidelines based on their non-binding nature, though they may certainly have an influence on the Commission's thinking as it drafts legislative proposals, indeed that was presumably the expectation.

COMMISSION v. EUROPEAN CENTRAL BANK
Case C-11/00, 2003 ECJ CELEX LEXIS 67, [2003] ECR I-7147

Note 1 (Both questions) — This judgment offers an insight into another aspect of "independence" for EU institutions — in this case independence from one another, as opposed to independence from influences outside the EU structure. The Court did not consider that the ECB's legally mandated independence was jeopardized. However, it is clear that that independence is to be interpreted strictly in terms of its role as the central bank in setting of monetary policy, and there is no reason why the Commission or its agencies should be excluded from an oversight role as regards internal ethics and fraud. In fact, it would make sense that such investigations would be carried out by an agency that was entirely independent of the Bank.

§ 13.03   ENFORCEMENT OF COMPETITION LAW

[A]   Regulatory Powers and Procedures Relating to Anticompetitive Conduct

REGULATION 1/2003
[2003] OJ L1/1

REGULATION 773/2004
[2004] OJ L 123/27)

Note 1 In the first place, the Commission needs judicial and police support to carry out inspections on companies' premises. The Member States also have a great deal of involvement in other aspects: (see in particular articles 11–16). It is particularly noteworthy that the Competition authorities of the Member States:

(a)   have the right to be consulted on proposed decisions and to participate in hearings of individual cases.

(b)   can withdraw the benefits of a block exemption for their territory (article 29(2)).

(c)   can participate in investigations (article 19(2))

(d)   can be required by the Commission to carry out investigations in their territory.

Note 2 These non-binding pronouncements had no legal effect, so they could not be relied on as such, but assuming the context and facts had not changed, they might have a claim based on a breach of the principle of legitimate expectations. (See further Chapter 17)

Note 3 Some have objected to the scope and severity of these powers, but their evolution reflects also an evolution in the much increased attention being given by the Member States to competition matters, particularly cartels. In some Member States, price fixing is now a criminal offence. Thus overall the Commission is no longer out ahead of national policy and it gains considerably legitimacy for it powers as a result. It should be kept in mind that the inspection powers are subject to both ECJ and national courts' controls.

Note 5 The "rights of the defence" frequently alluded to by the Courts (see the following cases) in this context are really the court's formulation of the EU's duty to make known to the parties the facts on which it will rely in its decision. It is in the interests of good decision-making that the parties be given the opportunity to comment; thus any facts relied on in a final decision that were not alleged in the Statement of Objections will likely invalidate the decision. Thus, the Court has to balance the Commission's limitations on how it can obtain proof against the need to ensure that it does not act in an arbitrary fashion. All of this might rather suggest that the Commission's Decisions are almost like the presentation of the prosecution case with a recommended fine. The parties almost invariably appeal and the CFI or even ultimately the ECJ decide. However, this is not a particularly accurate analogy, because the defence to the allegations has to be made at the stage between the Statement of Objections and the final Decision. After that, any Court review can focus only breach of EU law. The CFI has shown itself willing however to dig deep into the facts to make sure that the legal evaluation is properly based. See for example the *Alrosa* case in Chapter 17, *infra*.

[B]   The Standard and Burden of Proof

TOKAI CARBON CO. LTD (T-71/03), INTECH EDM BV (T-74/03), INTECH EDM AG (T-87/03) AND SGL CARBON AG (T-91/03) v. COMMISSION
Joined Cases T-71/03, T-74/03, T-87/03 and T-91/03, 2005 ECJ CELEX LEXIS 803, [2005] ECR II-10

SCHNEIDER ELECTRIC SA v. COMMISSION
Case T-310/01, 2002 ECJ CELEX LEXIS 424, [2002] ECR II-4071

Note 1 The rights of the defense concern all those procedural and evidentiary issues that secure for the parties involved the ability to present a fully informed response to the allegations and possible sanctions. Thus, the SO should be explicit and clear about which documents or statements are being relied on, what periods are involved, whether fines are likely to be imposed, which conduct specifically is considered to be a violation, and who led the cartel. Given the Commission's "judicial" role, holding it to these standards is vital if a viable policy is to be pursued.

In *Schneider*, it is instructive to follow the Court's analysis and the way in which it picked out inconsistencies and non sequiturs in the Commission's decision. This then highlights the essential purpose of the Statement of Objections (SO). It must, as the Court states, enable the parties to understand clearly what the Commission's allegations are so as to be able to respond to them. The final decision need not correspond to the SO but must be based on the file including the parties' responses; it cannot take off in a new direction not made known to the parties. In such a case a second statement of objections should be issued, which is essentially what the court ordered.

The Court's decision to annul the Commission's decision in the *Schneider* case was a significant step, since it rarely does so in the context of merger control. The CFI in 2007 found for Schneider in a damages action under article 288 arising out of the Commission's failures in the original decision.

[C]   The Scope of the Commission's Discretion in Deciding Whether to Take Action

AUTOMEC SRL v. COMMISSION
Case T-24/90, 1992 ECJ CELEX LEXIS 66, [1992] ECR II 2223

UNION FRANCAISE DE L'EXPRESS (UFEX), FORMERLY SYNDICAT FRANCAIS DE L'EXPRESS INTERNATIONAL (SFEI), DHL INTERNATIONAL AND SERVICE CRIE v. COMMISSION
Case C-119/97 P, 1999 ECJ CELEX LEXIS 250, [1999] ECR I-1341

Note 1 Q1 — The cases are not inconsistent. The essential difference was that in SFEI, the Commission was found to have overlooked an essential element of its review, namely that the effects of prior illegal conduct might still be felt.

Q2 — The ECJ and CFI in the respective cases set out a number of reasons that would justify the Commission's deciding not to act; these included:

(a)   the availability of proceedings in Member State courts
(b)   the more general actions to be undertaken by the Commission in the same area
(c)   the prior review of the merger involving the parties whose conduct was the subject of the applicants' complaint
(d)   the seriousness of the breaches of law
(e)   in the case of past conduct, the extent to which the effects of that conduct might still be felt

(f) the duration and extent of the infringements

(g) the existence of a block exemption

Note 2 The Court clearly takes the view, as already seen in the SFEI case, that the Commission's responsibility is not to look after the interests of individuals but the public interest as a whole.

Note 3 Subsidiarity would not be an appropriate basis because it rests on an entirely different premise, namely whether an action is better taken at the national level or the EU level. "Community Interest" is much wider and is based on many factors including the need to establish a principle, or the seriousness of the impact across the EU even if the conduct is only confined to one Member State. Regulation 1/2003 recognizes "Community Interest" but not subsidiarity. Moreover, this doctrine (as seen in Chapter 5) really has to do with legislation, not executive action.

SUMITOMO CHEMICAL CO. LTD, SUMIKA FINE CHEMICALS CO. LTD, v. COMMISSION
Joined Cases T-22/02 and T-23/02, 2005 ECJ CELEX LEXIS 468, [2005] ECR II-4065

Note 1 This dichotomy is a function of the administrative system as opposed to an adversarial court-based approach with which US lawyers would identify. In the administrative system the absence of a penalty is irrelevant where the public interest would be served by establishing the existence of the misconduct in itself. It would also have the practical impact for the company in question of making it a "recidivist" such that a second offence would trigger a larger fine (see below).

[D] Confidentiality

POSTBANK NV v. COMMISSION
Case T-353/94, 1996 ECJ CELEX LEXIS 93, [1996] ECR II-921

Note 1 The Court did not condemn the Commission's transmittal of the Statement of Objections to the national court, nor did it require the Commission to impose any conditions of confidentiality or restrictions on use. What the Court did find fault with was strictly a procedural failure to give the interested party the opportunity to make its views known before the Commission adopted the contested decision to hand over the documents.

Note 2 The different action could best be explained on the basis that the Court of Justice could not countenance laying down restrictions on the national courts. They should be trusted to use and protect information according to national law.

[E] Legal Privilege

AM & S EUROPE LIMITED v. COMMISSION
Case 155/79, 1982 ECJ CELEX LEXIS 15, [1982] ECR 1575

Notes 1 & 2 (All questions) — The doctrine described by the Court in this case is not really a manifestation of the Anglo-Saxon concept of legal privilege but rather an element of what the Court describes as the "rights of the defense." These rights (as already mentioned elsewhere) are intended to ensure that the administrative body complies with all evidentiary and procedural requirements so that its decision is legally supportable. Enabling parties to communicate confidentially with outside legal counsel is seen as an essential element in this context, while communications with in-house lawyers is not.

[F]   Fines and Remedies

REGULATION 1/2003
[2003] OJ L1/1

TOKAI CARBON CO. LTD, INTECH EDM BV, INTECH EDM AG, AND SGL CARBON AG v. COMMISSION
Joined Cases T-71/03, T-74/03, T-87/03 and T-91/03, 2005 ECJ CELEX LEXIS 803, [2005] ECR II-10

Note 1 Q1 — The Court would not substitute its own judgment for that of the Commission but it will analyze the decision to make sure that the Commission has given adequate reasons and that those reasons are substantiated by the facts it has relied on. Thus in *Tokai* it rejected arguments that:

(a)   Tokai was fined twice for the same conduct;
(b)   The separation of the investigation into three separate proceedings for different products or different time frames was an improper way to increase the fines;
(c)   The fines were not proportionate to the respective parties' turnover;
(d)   The guidelines under which they were calculated were introduced after the conduct had ended and should not have been applied;
(e)   The factors taken into account in calculating turnover were improper because they were adjusted for global market shares;
(f)   Inadequate reductions were given under the leniency notice.

Q2 — Interestingly, the Court, in addition to denying all these arguments, also took the position that it could not substitute its own judgment for the Commission's because it would then be imposing fines without having given other parties the ability to review and comment on its reasoning.

Note 2 (All questions) — Although the application of heavier penalties based on new guidelines may look retroactive and therefore suspect, there is actually no good reason why the parties should benefit from a lighter penalty just because they thought they could get away with less at the time of the conduct.

§ 13.04   DUTIES OF THE MEMBER STATES IN IMPLEMENTING EU ACTION

[A]   The Nature of the Duty

COMMISSION v. FRANCE
(FRENCH SEAMEN)
Case 167/73, [1974] ECR 359

Note 1 The ECJ determined that the uncertainty created by the existence of laws, even though not followed in practice, was a violation of the Treaty.

Note 2 See *Commission v. Netherlands,* Case 96/81 [1982] ECR 1791, where administrative practices were found to be insufficient to implement a directive; but compare *Commission v. Germany,* 29/84, [1985] ECR 1661, where an administrative practice that could not be changed without publicity and a certain degree of formality was held to be insufficient to fulfil Germany's obligation to implement the so-called "nurses directive".

It is possible that the "directly applicable" argument might succeed where the Member State had no legislation on the subject matter of the directive — in the United Kingdom by virtue of the European Communities Act, the EU measure would in any event have the force of law (see Chapter 5).

The French government persistently failed to comply with the judgment in case 167/

73 and also adopted French citizenship requirements for ownership of vessels — a situation somewhat similar to that in *Factortame*: see *Commission v. French Republic* Case C-334/94, [1996] ECR 1307.

COMMISSION v. ITALY
(INSPECTION CHARGES)
Case C-129/00, 2003 ECJ CELEX LEXIS 77, [2003] ECR I-14637

Note 1 The Court was careful to avoid a conclusion that the Italian courts themselves were responsible for the breach by Italy. Instead it held the legislature and executive responsible for maintaining in force legislation that permitted the courts to follow a line of precedent that breached Community law, in this case by throwing up a number of evidentiary and procedural barriers that made the recovery of illegal charges almost impossible.

ROQUETTE FRERES SA v. DIRECTEUR GENERAL DE LA CONCURRENCE, DE LA CONSOMMATION ET DE LA REPRESSION DES FRAUDES, AND COMMISSION
Case C-94/00, 2002 ECJ CELEX LEXIS 270, [2002] ECR I-9011

Note 1 There is some very delicate interplay here between EU and national requirements. Given the Court's conclusions mentioned in the *Hoechst* case, any questions of a fundamental rights nature would have to be reviewed solely under EU law.

Note 2 As the *Roquette* case indicates (which would still be good law today despite the repeal of Regulation 17), the Commission should not use its inspection powers based on pure whim. This would certainly raise "search and seizure" issues.

Note 3 The point of course is that EU law is entirely dependent on national authorization for its execution. To the extent these authorities are subject to judicial review there is no reason why a party should not *under national law* assert national law rights with respect to the actions of the state authorities. However, this could not be allowed to interfere with the legitimate needs of the EU system.

[B] Rights of Private Parties to Compel the Commission to Take Action

STAR FRUIT COMPANY SA v. COMMISSION
Case 247/87, 1989 ECJ CELEX LEXIS 140, [1989] ECR 291

Note 1 The Commission has a legal duty to protect the Treaties and EU legislation. Thus its interest is already established.

Note 2 Such an obligation would be purely based on political pressure, since there is not legal mechanism to force the Commission to act. Individuals might still have a Community action through Article 234, while an aggrieved Member State has independent standing to bring an action against another Member State.

Note 3 It would be open to Star Fruit to invoke EU legislation in opposition to the national rules in the national Courts under article 241.

COMMISSION v. ITALY
(MINIMUM PRICES)
Case 7/61, [1961] ECR 317

Note 1 The Commission's role as guardian of the Treaties means that it could use such proceedings to establish a point of law that would be in the general interest of legal certainty or the preservation of the Community interest. This is similar to its duty as discussed above in the *Sumimoto* case.

[C]   Do the Member States have "Rights of the Defense"?

COMMISSION v. BELGIUM
(MINERVAL)
Case 293/85, 1988 ECJ CELEX LEXIS 35, [1988] ECR 305

Note 1 The Court does refer to the dual purposes of the preliminary proceeding: one of which to give the State the right to defend itself. However, this was really a recognition that the interest of EU law are better served by making sure that all the relevant facts are heard. It does not suggest any kind of fundamental right that should be protected for reasons related to fundamental rights.

[D]   Remedies

COMMISSION v. GERMANY
(AIDS TO COAL PRODUCING REGIONS)
Case 70/72, [1973] ECR 813

Note 1 There seems no reason why the powers of the Commission could not extend also to Article 227 proceedings but it would normally not be necessary to take 'retroactive' measures because the underlying purpose is to bring an end to an infringement. Exceptionally, under Article 88, for example, the only way to end the infringement is to require repayment (or other action in relation to individuals) because, otherwise, the adverse effects of the conduct will continue.

The Court's orders themselves simply confirm the Commission's right to adopt the decision. Such decisions might then be invocable in the national courts under the general doctrine of invocability (direct effect) or Article 5.

The rationale for requiring "private citizens" to bear the cost of the Member State's breach seems to be that they would be able to challenge the Commission's decision against the illegal aid. The parties might then be able to claim damages, presumably from the Member State concerned, citing *Fives Lille Cail v. High Authority*, Joined Cases 19, 21/60, 2, 3/61, [1961] ECR 296.

COMMISSION v. FRANCE
(FISHERIES INSPECTIONS)
Case C-304/02, 2005 ECJ CELEX LEXIS 322, [2005] ECR I-6263

Note 1 Seriousness, duration and deterrent effect, applied to the gross domestic product (ability to pay) — these appear quite reminiscent of the fining violations for individuals for competition law infringements. The Court added that account should also be taken of the effects on private and Community interests.

Note 2 For specific breaches, financial penalties might seem appropriate. For more widespread activity, such as a breakdown in democracy or human rights in a Member State, which would involve the more general obligation to subscribe to the goals of the Treaty, political pressure would be the more appropriate remedy — as indeed happened some years ago when Austria elected a far-right government.

Note 3 The Commission would have to make this assessment, presumably based on some concrete actions to be taken by the French government.

§ 13.05   REPRESENTATION OF THE UNION IN EXTERNAL RELATIONS

COMMISSION v. COUNCIL
(AETR/ERTA)
Case 22/70, [1971] ECR 263

Note 1 (All questions) — The questions here highlight the tensions that exist between the Member States and the Commission over responsibilities to manage foreign affairs. As the EU has developed, and as monetary union became a reality, the Member States have tried to maintain control by denying the Commission a role. From an external point of view however, both act in the name of the EU, and as a practical matter this does not seem to have created problems for other countries.

FRANCE v. COMMISSION
(COMPETITION LAW ENFORCEMENT COOPERATION)
Case 327/91, 1994 ECJ CELEX LEXIS 26, [1994] ECR I-3641

Note 2 The problem so often faced by the Court is to ensure that the precarious but complex legal structure of the EC is not jeopardized even by relatively minor issues that nonetheless involve questions of principle. Here the principle is the role of the Council, clearly a major *political* issue. The Court's conclusions therefore should not be surprising.

Note 3 (All questions) — Representation by different 'institutions' does not seem at all unusual if one equates this with normal states' practice where negotiations are carried on by the government department or minister responsible for the particular subject matter.

Note 4 The Commission under the EC Treaty plays a true executive role in negotiating agreements. The most interesting aspect of the TEU Title VI articles is the assignment of responsibilities to the "Presidency" of the Council which look very much like executive duties — representing the Union and steering policy within the Council. This is however really a spokesman role than an executive one. Instead one should look to the High Representative for the executive function and in this regard, note again the changes that will come about as a result of the Reform Treaty and in particular the High Representative's position as a Commission Vice President as well as chair of the Council (in Foreign Affairs). This seems to be analogous to a parliamentary system of government, where the "executive" (*i.e.* the Vice President of the Commission) gets to be at the same time a part of the "legislature".

Chapter 14
JUDICIAL CONTROL

§ 14.02 STANDING

[A] "Another Person"

PLAUMANN & CO. v. COMMISSION
Case 25/62, [1963] ECR 95

Note 1. A decision addressed to a Member State will, in some contexts such as here, have a generalized effect on individuals since it authorizes the Member State to take action. Paradoxically, by recognizing the EU actions of this kind as "decisions addressed to another person", the Court opened up the possibility of an expansive scope for individual standing. This however was effectively shut down by its interpretation of direct and individual concern. The comment regarding the need not to interpret "restrictively" seems very much at odds with subsequent developments.

[B] Direct Concern

TOEPFER ET AL v. COMMISSION
Joined Cases 106 and 107/63, [1965] ECR 405

Note 1 The court considered that the decision was of direct concern because there was no need for any intervening act by any other authority. Once the decision was adopted, it had an immediate legal effect on the applicants.

Note 2 There is no such acknowledgement but, as already seen in Chapter 13, it would not be entirely incorrect to characterize the Member States' roles in this way, particularly as the Court's jurisprudence has developed.

Note 3 Although Article 230 only permits challenges to decisions, it recognizes that a regulation could be a disguised decision (see chapter 3). Thus the choice of measure ought not to have an adverse impact on standing. As will be seen later, the requirement that the act be characterized as a "decision" seems to have evaporated. (*Codorniu* et seq). Note the changes that will come about when the Treaty of Lisbon comes into effect.

INFRONT WM AG v. COMMISSION
Case T-33/01, 2005 ECJ CELEX LEXIS 691, [2005] ECR II-5897

Note 1 The Commission's letter (which it will be recalled from chapter 3, was ruled by the Court to be a "decision") had the legal effect of triggering mutual recognition obligations of the other Member States — only from that moment would they be required to recognize the U.K.'s designation of the coverage as of national interest. However, if the decision were not to change the applicant's position because its adoption made no difference to that position, then it could not have claimed to be directly concerned.

COMITE CENTRAL D'ENTREPRISE DE LA SOCIETE GENERALE DES GRANDES SOURCES AND OTHERS v. COMMISSION
Case T-96/92, 1995 ECJ CELEX LEXIS 27, [1995] ECR II-1213

Note 1 The Court determined that the only basis on which the Commission's decision could be considered of direct concern to the applicants was if the applicants' procedural rights under Regulation 4069/89, Article 18(4) had been violated. Thus, in the first place, there was clearly no general right to challenge just because the applicants' rights to be consulted under the Transfer of Understandings Directive or the potential adverse effect on their funds resulting from a reduction in the workforce were affected — these effects resulted from the merger itself and the effects of Member State legislation and not from the decision to approve the merger. In fact, the Court concluded that their procedural rights had not been violated.

[C]   Individual Concern in the Context of Decisions Addressed to Member States

TOEPFER ET AL v. COMMISSION
Joined Cases 106 and 107/63, [1965] ECR 405

PLAUMANN & CO. v. COMMISSION
Case 25/62, [1963] ECR 95

Note 1 The key difference between the two cases is that in *Plaumann*, anybody who might import the products was affected, while in *Toepfer*, the decision affected only those who *had* imported the products between certain dates. They were therefore in a closed class.

KWEKERIJ GEBROEDERS VAN DER KOOY BV ET AL v. COMMISSION
Joined Cases 67–68/85 and 70/85, [1988] ECR 219

Note 1 Q1–3 — The growers were obviously affected but did not qualify as a closed class. Note that the Court uses the same language in defining individual concern that it used to define regulations (see chapter 3).

Q4 — This case signals one of several expansions of the notion of individual concern. The growers' association would have been regarded as simply a collective of the growers themselves, who were held (consistent with the *Plaumann* approach) not to be individually concerned. However, the Court recognizes that the Association, given its special role, was affected in a number of ways that differed from the individual growers. Perhaps the ECJ saw the desirability of allowing only the Association to challenge, precisely because it would avoid a multiplicity of lawsuits while still allowing judicial control.

Note 2 The Association was the collective negotiator of gas tariffs and so had an interest independent of the individual growers. It was also a party to the contract that contained the invalidated tariff.

[D]   Individual Concern in the Context of Decisions Addressed to Another Individual

METRO SB-GROSSMÄRKTE GMBH & C. KG v. COMMISSION
Case 26/76, [1977] ECR 1875

Note 1 The reasoning in the *Metro* case was a rather abrupt departure from previous decisions. The Court stated only that "it is in the interests of a satisfactory administration of justice and of the proper application of Articles 85 [81] and 86 [82]" that applicants should have standing.

Note 2 (All questions) — The applicant here clearly was unique in that it had made the complaint that led to the decision, but it is hard to see how it differed from any other dealer who might also have been affected. It thus appears that the executive nature of such decisions justifies a more expansive approach to individual concern. One of the reasons for the different treatment may well be that decisions addressed to Member States are subject to judicial challenge by any Member State. While this is true also of decisions addressed to individuals, it is very unlikely that a Member State would want to take action.

KRUIDVAT BVBA v. COMMISSION
Case C-70/97 P, 1998 ECJ CELEX LEXIS 617, [1998] ECR I-7183

Note 1 Unlike Metro, Kruidvat had not filed a complaint with the Commission. However, it was involved in a lawsuit where the legality of its agreement was in issue. The Court considered that it was adequately protected because the legality of the agreement could be reviewed by the national court. Overall it seems therefore that the Court will continue to take a very restrictive approach to the concept of individual concern. Except for the fact that *Kwekerij* concerned a decision addressed to a Member State, the cases do appear analogous in most respects.

Note 2 A formal complaint prior to the decision might have been sufficient provided it was not obviously a contrivance to gain standing.

[E] Individual Concern in the Context of Challenges to Regulations

ALLIED CORPORATION v. COMMISSION
Joined Cases 239/82, 275/82, [1984] ECR 1005

CODORNIU SA v. COUNCIL
Case 309/89, 1994 ECJ CELEX LEXIS 4, [1994] ECR I-1853

Note 1 In *Allied*, the ECJ did not attempt to define its view on whether the measure challenged constituted a bundle of disguised decisions; however, it could certainly be so viewed from a practical standpoint given that the applicants found to have standing belonged to a class that was "closed" — no other companies' products could be the subject of the specific duties imposed. Probably the reason for avoiding the characterization issue lay in the fact that the legislation could legally be only in the form of a regulation — there is no provision for the adoption of decisions. The case is thus actually largely consistent with the narrow construction of "direct and individual concern" found in the cases following. (*Toepfer*, etc.)

Note 2 In *Allied*, the effect of the challenged regulation, No. 1976/82 as amended, was that antidumping duties were imposed on the products of three companies: Allied, Transcontinental, and Kaiser, which had taken part in the investigations.

Another company, Demufert, was an importer which acted as agent for Allied's products. It was not named in the subject regulations. Demufert was found to be neither individually concerned — being in a general category of importers — not directly concerned because the existence of the dumping was established by reference to U.S. export prices, not European retail prices, so Demufert was not "implicated", i.e., capable of commenting on or able to rectify the actions taken by its U.S. supplier.

By contrast in *Extramet Industrie v. Council*, Case C-358/89, 1992 ECJ CELEX LEXIS 59, [1991] ECR I-2501, the Court ruled that a dumping measure may be of individual concern to certain importers. Such importers might include those who are referred to in the contested measures, as where the level of duty is established partly by reference to the resale price charged by the importer; or the importer is the most important importer of the product, the ultimate consumer of it, and particularly dependent upon it for its business.

Note 3 The ability to challenge legislation in the national courts may have been some guarantee for Demufert, but it was not considered by the ECJ to be relevant to the specific question of its standing under Article 230. The Commission's observation was relevant therefore only to provide some assurance that the exclusion of admissibility for importers did not deprive them of all remedies.

Note 4 In *Codorniu*, what is most noticeable is the complete absence of any attempt to characterize the regulation as a decision, which quite clearly it was not. In looking at individual concern, the ground that "differentiated" Codorniu from all other traders was that it would be unable in the future to derive economic benefit from a graphic trademark it had used since 1924. The differentiating factor thus was the loss of the ability to exploit a valuable property right. There seems no reason why in principle there could not be other claimants with other unique situations (e.g. a party with a contract that it would no longer be able to honor) so the individuality of the effect seems to have broadened to include any party with a unique pre-acquired right. This case therefore was seen as a sign of a changed attitude to standing, which however turned out not to be the case more generally, as the next case indicates.

COMMISSION v. JEGO-QUERE & CIE SA
Case C-263/02 P, 2004 ECJ CELEX LEXIS 157, [2004] ECR I-3425

Note 1 Q1 — While the ECJ overturned the CFI's expansive reading of Article 230, its approach was a good deal more transparent than had been evident in the earlier decisions, since it sought to explain at length how the applicants' rights were protected through the ability to challenge regulations by pleading their illegality in the national courts. The absence of a legal path for the applicants to do so in France should not be considered relevant, since it was actually the duty of the French government to assure such procedure existed.

Q2 — The ECJ and CFI seem to be on different wavelengths probably due to their different roles. The CFI sees its duty to be to make sure that the administration follows the right procedures and behaves in a transparent fashion. It has this role of course in competition matters and thus tends to see the Commission as an administrative agency requiring such supervision. It does not see that this approach threatens the discretionary powers of the Commission precisely because the control is procedural and not substantive.

One might, on the other hand, interpret the ECJ's stance as recognizing a broader dimension to the question of standing. As a form of sovereign power, the EU should not be exposed to challenges from individuals when adopting legislation, any more than it is possible for citizens to sue Congress directly for adopting unconstitutional acts. The proper course of action is to raise the subject as an incident in a true case or controversy. This can arise in the EU through the article 234 procedure.

[F]   Decisions Not to Act and Failure to Act

EUROPEAN PARLIAMENT v. COUNCIL
(TRANSPORT POLICY)
Case 13/83, [1985] ECR 1513

Note 1 See para 36 of the Judgment. Under article 232 (unlike article 230) the Parliament, as an institution of the EU, had always had a right to bring an action. (It now does have such a right under article 230 also.) However, it had to show that the Council had actually failed to act, which meant determining whether or not it had adopted a transport policy. The Court found implicitly that even a decision not to do so was still a policy. More generally it found that it was impossible to determine a failure where there was a broad measure of discretion. Thus, on the broad ground, the Parliament was unsuccessful. On the narrow ground of failure to take steps required to be taken before the end of the transitional period however, the Court upheld its complaint.

LORD BETHELL v. COMMISSION
Case 246/81, [1982] ECR 2277

Notes 1 Q1 — The key point made by the ECJ here is that the applicant was not demanding that action be taken with respect to him personally but that an inquiry be opened into industry practices generally. Although no doubt he himself was a consumer of airline services, there was no way to distinguish him from such consumers in general.

Q2 — It seems that the right to challenge an action under Article 232 and the right to challenge an action under Article 230 are subject to the same conditions of admissibility — see the *T-Mobile* case below.

Q3 — Had the applicant been, say, another airline that was suffering losses as a result of Commission inaction, it might have been successful in a challenge under Article 232 because it could have challenged a decision under Article 230 exonerating other airlines from liability for infringement of Articles 81 and 82. Such a challenge might be possible in very exceptional circumstances, where the applicant would have had standing to challenge a regulation under Article 230. However, in these cases, the only persons with standing would seem to be the parties who are analogous to addressees of a decision, so third parties who might be affected by the regulation would still have no standing.

COMMISSION v. T-MOBILE AUSTRIA GMBH
Case C-141/02 P, 2005 ECJ CELEX LEXIS 728, [2005] ECR I-1283

Note 1 This was an article 230 proceeding but was based on a complaint that the Commission by its letter addressed to T-Mobile had failed to take action. Compared with the previous history of such cases, the CFI had apparently taken the limited exception noted by the ECJ and developed it into a broader principle allowing applicants admissibility where they were complaining about a decision *not* to act. The CFI had held the action admissible based on the reasoning in paragraphs 16–21, but the ECJ insisted that a challenge could only be brought if the challenged act produced legal effects, which it considered it not to have done. There had to be *a legal requirement to act*, but there was not, since this was entirely a matter within the Commission's discretion. The result of this decision is that article 232 is essentially aligned with article 230 where the decision in question is the refusal to act.

§ 14.03   CHALLENGES UNDER ARTICLE 241 ("PLEA OF ILLEGALITY")

SIMMENTHAL S.P.A. v. COMMISSION
Case 92/78, [1979] ECR 777

Note 1 The Applicant was seeking to challenge not only underlying regulations but also the "notices". However article 241 only refers to regulations. The ECJ concluded that if the notices were part of the regulatory scheme it should be possible to challenge them also.

§ 14.04   RIPENESS AND JUSTICIABILITY

[A]   Non-Existent Acts

CONSORZIO COOPERATIVE D'ABRUZZO v. COMMISSION
Case 15/85, 1987 ECJ CELEX LEXIS 135, [1987] ECR 1005

Note 1 A non-existent act would not be subject to the time limits for challenge in Article 230 because, as a preliminary matter, the Court could find that there was never an act, the date of which could start time running.

Note 2 Since the Court speaks of a "serious and manifest error" one would expect the act to demonstrate on its face — and be obvious, therefore to the world — that it was improper.

The use of the "non-existence" concept has not been widespread and indeed seems unnecessary where the act can be annulled under Article 173 (or the equivalent articles under the other treaties). However, where the act in question is *not* an act that is challengeable, a finding of non-existence amounts to the only recourse that the applicant has against it. This could therefore be important because it opens up the possibility of attacking EU actions which have serious effects for individuals but fall short of constituting "acts" of the institution. This is an area that is worthy of further exploration by litigants.

In *Commission v. BASF and Others*, Case T-79/89, [1992] ECR II-315, the CFI had declared a Commission action non-existent, but the ECJ annulled that conclusion (Case 137/92 P, 1994 ECJ CELEX LEXIS 112, [1994] ECR I-2555) and held instead that the action was in breach of an essential procedural requirement:

> "47 Relying on the judgment of the Court of Justice in Case 15/85 Consorzio Cooperative d' Abruzzo v. Commission 1987 ECR 1005, the Commission points out that the irregularities in question, assuming that they may be regarded as such, concern only the internal procedure for drawing up the contested decision, so that its addressees could not have identified them merely by reading the text which had been duly notified to them. The alleged irregularities were therefore not sufficiently obvious for the contested decision to be treated as non-existent.

> 48 It should be remembered that acts of the Community institutions are in principle presumed to be lawful and accordingly produce legal effects, even if they are tainted by irregularities, until such time as they are annulled or withdrawn.

> 49 However, by way of exception to that principle, acts tainted by an irregularity whose gravity is so obvious that it cannot be tolerated by the Community legal order must be treated as having no legal effect, even provisional, that is to say that they must be regarded as legally non-existent. The purpose of this exception is to maintain a balance between two fundamental, but sometimes conflicting, requirements with which a legal order must comply, namely stability of legal relations and respect for legality.

> 50 From the gravity of the consequences attaching to a finding that an act of a Community institution is non-existent it is self-evident that, for reasons of legal certainty, such a finding is reserved for quite extreme situations."

Note 4 It may be recalled that the purpose of allowing actions under 226 is to establish a principle — the Commission has a legitimate interest in doing this. There is no legitimate interest served in annulling an individual decision that has been corrected.

[B]   Actions Preliminary to a Decision

INTERNATIONAL BUSINESS MACHINES CORPORATION v. COMMISSION
Case 60/81, 1992 ECJ CELEX LEXIS 27, [1981] ECR 2639

Note 1 Perhaps the most interesting part of this judgment is the penultimate paragraph, which refers to exceptional circumstances where the action complained of is so lacking in legality that it might be appropriate to allow an action. Conceivably what the ECJ had in mind here was the "non-existent act" concept similar to the situation regarding the first of the opinions in the *Societe des Usines a Tubes de la Sarre* case. However, it is clear that this will be a very unusual situation indeed. In less severe cases, one can see merit in the Court's approach, in that it should normally be expected that the facts will only come to light as the result of the completion of the full procedures — any early decision would be considered premature and would seriously impede the Commission's performance of its duties. The circumstances under which an SO itself might be subject to review could perhaps be that it named the wrong party, or contained a manifest error of fact that undermined the whole position of the Commission. The addressee would after all be put to considerable expense in responding, and if it was clear from the outset that the Commission would lose, why should the applicant have to wait?

[C]   Scope of Review

UNITED KINGDOM v. COUNCIL
(WORKING TIME DIRECTIVE)
Case C-84/94, 1996 ECJ CELEX LEXIS 194, [1996] ECR I-5755

Note 1 Q1 — It would be impossible for the Court to become involved in making substantive appraisals of discretionary acts since it has no means of gathering evidence or factual background to enable it to do so. The grounds of review are clearly designed to exclude such a review and focus on the satisfaction of procedural requirements, truthfulness and adequate reasoning.

Q2 — It could actually be regarded as more suggestive of the opposite view. The ECJ does not consider it appropriate to assess political decisions. It acts more as a constitutional court and thus will evaluate acts for compliance with fundamental rights and with procedural requirements only.

ORGANISATION DES MODJAHEDINES DU PEUPLE D'IRAN v. COUNCIL
Case T-228/02, [2006 ECR] NYR

Note 1 As was evident in the context of Competition law enforcement (*supra*, chapter 13), the EU Courts generally draw a very defined scope of review: they will look at the reasoning of a decision to ensure that it is supported by the facts — so similar to the U.S. procedure. There must obviously be adequate reasons stated to enable them to match the decision to the facts.

[D]   Acts Internal to an Institution

JEAN-CLAUDE MARTINEZ, CHARLES DE GAULLE, FRONT NATIONAL AND
EMMA BONINO AND OTHERS v. PARLIAMENT
Joined Cases T-222/99, T-327/99 and T-329/99, 2001 ECJ CELEX LEXIS 468, [2001] ECR II-2823

Note 1 The Court's decision clearly adopts an extremely narrow view of what constitutes an internal act. The only "external" parties affected here were members of the Parliament.

Note 2 (All questions) — In the U.S. such matters would be considered purely practical and pertaining to the legislative branch. No such distinction exists in the EU. The European approach is certainly more reminiscent of an administrative review. Article 230 was originally so conceived, so it does not then seem a stretch to interpret it as concerning such situations.

[E]   Delegated Acts

DIR INTERNATIONAL FILM SRL AND OTHERS v. COMMISSION
Joined Cases T-369/84 and T-85/95, 1998 ECJ CELEX LEXIS 23, [1998] ECR II-357

Note 1 The difficulty for an individual in such a case would be to establish that the act challenged was in fact an EU decision. There is no acceptance (yet) that the Member States, in any formal sense, act as and extension of the institutions of the EU.

[F]   Matters Outside the Jurisdictional Boundaries of the Treaties

THERMENHOTEL STOISER FRANZ GESELLSCHAFT MBH & CO. KG AND OTHERS v. COMMISSION
Case T-158/99, 2004 ECJ CELEX LEXIS 731, [2004] ECR II-1

Note 1 One can draw the conclusion from the Court's remarks here that just because an act might be outside the jurisdiction of the EU does not make it any less an act of the EU, subject, all other things being equal, to challenge under Article 230. It is either legal or not, and the question is no different than it would be for any other form of challenge.

ORGANISATION DES MODJAHEDINES DU PEUPLE D'IRAN, v. COUNCIL
Case T-228/02, [20..] ECR NYR

Note 1 Q1 — This case illustrates the differences between acts under the TEU and acts under the EC Treaty. The EU Courts will certainly examine any act to determine whether it trespasses on the jurisdiction of the EC Treaty but it is not entirely clear what consequences this might have if found to be the case. Such a decision could be considered a form of judicial review of TEU acts, but with only a very limited outcome if found to be properly adopted under the TEU.

Q2 — The case highlights the practical difficulty of providing for different degrees of judicial control based on the subject matter. It seems inevitable that at some point some form of rationalization will have to occur, perhaps based on a concept of separation of administrative and political acts.

§ 14.05   EFFECTS OF ANNULMENT

[A]   The Relationship of Standing to the Scope of an Annulment

NTN TOYO BEARING COMPANY LIMITED AND OTHERS v. COUNCIL
Case 240/84, 1987 ECJ CELEX LEXIS 474, [1987] ECR 1809

Note 1 In the *NTN* case, the ECJ did suggest that the whole regulation might be void, but the limited standing of the applicants made a complete annulment impossible. This seems a strange result until one realizes that the basis of individual challenge, particularly as regards regulations, is very distinctly the interest of the applicant because of the effect on it. An applicant who has standing but does not choose to challenge an act has demonstrated that it is not concerned. On the other hand, a challenge to a decision under the competition rules by a third party could result in the whole decision being annulled, thus benefiting others who have not challenged.

Note that in *Regina v. Ministry of Agriculture, Fisheries and Food ex. p. H&R Ecroyd Holdings and John Rupert Ecroyd*, Case C-127/94 1996 ECJ CELEX LEXIS 204, [1996] ECR I-2731, the Court held that a judgment annulling legislation in a complex field (milk quota legislation) does not give individuals the right to disapply similar legislation in other cases.

Note 2 The answer really depends on the act in question. A failure to follow a required procedure for a specific decision would inevitably call in question the entire decision. At the same time, it would be remedied by going through the process again, correctly.

The ability to annul an EU act *in part* is explicitly recognized by the Treaty. This is a discretion vested in the ECJ which has to take into account whether the provision is truly severable. See also *Transocean Marine Point Association v. Commission*, Case

17/74 [1974] ECR 1063. For an example of a case where partial annulment was not possible, see *Jamet v. Commission*, Case 37/71, [1972] ECR 483.

[B] The Scope of Actions Required to Cure the Defect in the Annulled Act

ROGER TREMBLAY, HARRY KESTENBERG AND SYNDICAT DES EXPLOITANTS DE LIEUX DE LOISIRS (SELL) v. COMMISSION
Case T-224/95, 1997 ECJ CELEX LEXIS 97 [1997] ECR II-2215

Note 1 The Commission must pay attention to the whole judgment and then rectify the precise procedural mistakes found the Court. In this case this did not entail carrying out an investigation but merely giving reasons for its previous decision.

§ 14.06 CLAIMS FOR DAMAGES AGAINST EU INSTITUTIONS

[A] Tort Liability?

CLAUDE SAYAG AND S.A. ZURICH v. JEAN-PIERRE LEDUC, DENISE THONNON AND S.A. LA CONCORDE
Case 9/69, [1969] ECR 329

Note 1 The concept explained by the Court in *Sayag*, is rather hard to understand for common lawyers. Essentially, EU liability for damages is limited to those cases where the action causing damage is part of the tasks entrusted to the institutions. Driving a car is not such a case — although exceptionally it might be, where the institution had required it as an integral part of its duties.

Note 2 Q1 — The proper remedy for the injured party would be to sue in the domestic courts. If immunity is claimed, the Institution can be requested to waive the immunity. If such waiver is declined, an action could be brought under Article 230 to challenge that decision. (See the Privileges and Immunities Protocol in the Documentary Supplement.)

The Article 288 concept is not equivalent to an action in tort. It is an administrative law remedy designed to help ensure compliance by the administration with the legal limitations on the exercise of power.

Q2 — it is possible to see a systematic approach to the subject. Where the act is truly an exercise of power by an EU institution subject to legal limitations, a plea of immunity in the domestic courts would be appropriate, and the remedy should be sought in the ECJ. Where, on the other hand, the act is purely incidental to an exercise of power, no immunity should be claimed — and a refusal to waive such immunity ought to be challengeable before the ECJ.

Note 3 (All questions) — In the U.S. Constitution there are no provisions comparable to Article 288 of the EC Treaty. Rather, the individual who seeks to recover damages for the commission of unconstitutional acts from the federal government has to overcome the doctrine of sovereign immunity. Absent the waiver of sovereign immunity the federal government is immune from suit. Such waivers of sovereign immunity have usually been effected by statute. The primary example would be the Federal Torts Claims Act, 28 U.S.C.A. sections 2671 et seq. This waiver is far from an unqualified or universal submission to liability. On the contrary this legislation created a complex structure with many exceptions, which has given rise to much litigation. In general Congress has been cautious in waiving the sovereign immunity of the federal government.

As to the internment of persons of Japanese origin during World War II, this was upheld against constitutional attack in one of the most controversial decisions in the Supreme Court's history: *Koretmatsu v. United States*, 323 U.S. 214 (1944). In recognition of the injustice done, Congress passed legislation authorizing ex gratia payments to the survivors of the internment camps.

ISMERI EUROPA SRL v. COURT OF AUDITORS
Case T-277/97, 1999 ECJ CELEX LEXIS 131, [1999] ECR II-1825

Note 1 As indicated in the notes to *Sayag*, it is misleading to speak in terms of tort actions here. The EU Courts do not have jurisdiction to decide what are essentially civil law matters. Their role is really to serve as an administrative court and thus they approach all such matters on the basis of evaluation of the propriety of the administrative act.

[B] Claims Arising from Legislation or Decision-Making in Implementation of EU Policy

HOLTZ & WILLEMSEN GMBH v. COUNCIL AND COMMISSION
Case 153/73, [1974] ECR 675

Note 1 Where the claim relates to legislation or decision-making, the breach must be of a rule of law intended for the protection of individuals such as the principles of proportionality, legitimate expectations or equality, or procedural rules such as *ne bis in idem*. For example, see: *Zuckerfabrik Schoppenstedt v. Council*, Case 5/71, [1971] ECR 975; *Bayerische HNL Vermehrungsbetriebe GmbH v. Council and Commission*, Joined Cases 83, 94/76, 4, 15, 40/77 [1978] ECR1209; *Amylum and Tunnel Refineries v. Council and Commission*, Joined Cases 116, 124/77, [1979] ECR 3497. For a successful claim, see *Mulder v. Minister van Landbouw en Visserij*, Case C-120/86, [1988] ECR 2321 (legitimate expectations).

In this case, A-G Capotorti distinguished three elements:

(1)   the level of importance of the infringed rule;
(2)   the degree of blame to be attributed to the author of the measure;
(3)   the extent of the loss suffered.

A mere technical error may result in annulment but not damages: *Asteris v. Commission*, Joined Cases 194-206/83, [1985] ECR 2815.

Note 2 (All questions) — The discrimination principle was certainly relevant and as the Court indicated, had the measure been anything other than a short term transitional one, it should have been a cause for an award of damages.

Note 3 There is no such requirement. However, the act in question itself must be the direct cause of the damage.

The causal link required must be direct: see *Compagnie Continental v. France*, Case 169/73 [1975] ECR 135; *Acieries du Temple of High Authority*, Case 36/62, [1962] ECR 296; *Dumortier Freres SA v. Council*, Joined Cases 64 and 113/76, 167 and 239/78, 27, 28 and 45/79, [1982] ECR 1733.

COMMISSION v. CAMAR SRL AND TICO SRL
Case C-312/00 P, 2002 ECJ CELEX LEXIS 338, [2002] ECR I-11355

Note 1 The Court did not make any explicit reference to a superior rule of law, but instead relied on the manifest error of appraisal by the Commission. However, this itself could be considered the superior rule of law, namely a flagrant disregard of the limits placed on its discretion. In other words, the requirement to behave within the limits of the allowed discretion is a rule that exists for the protection of individuals and a wilful disregard of it brings the action within the scope of the *Holtz* rule.

[C]   Claims Based on Maladministration

HANS-MARTIN TILLACK v. COMMISSION
Case T-193/04, 2006 ECJ CELEX LEXIS 553, [2006] ECR II-3995

Note 1 The Court took the view that the Commission was exercising a discretion here but this is obviously very different from a discretion relating to a choice of legislative policy. It is difficult to understand why one would not simply evaluate the act based on whether there had been a breach of a fundamental right or a "due process" right without regard to whether the act was in some way a discretionary one.

[D]   Claims Not Involving an Illegal Act — Equality of Burden

SA BIOVILAC NV v. EUROPEAN ECONOMIC COMMUNITY
Case 59/83, [1984] ECR 4057

Note 1 (All questions) — The equivalent concept under the U.S. Constitution would be the takings clauses of the Fifth and Fourteenth Amendments. It would arise in a case where a private property owner claimed that a government regulation imposed such a special and unequal burden on his property that it constituted a taking of his property for which he was due just compensation. Such arguments have sometimes enjoyed success before the Supreme Court. See, for example, *Dolan v. City of Tigard*, 114 S.Ct. 2309 (1994).

It is likely that claims of this kind will only succeed on an exceptional basis because of the conditions set by the Court. See *Compagnie d'Approvisionnement v. Commission*, Joined Cases 9 and 11/71, [1972] ECR 391; and *Compagnie Continentale France v. Council*, Case 169/73, [1975] ECR 117. As the Court indicated in *Biovilac*, if this proposition were to be accepted, the burden on the applicant to prove that the damage it suffered "exceeds the limits of the economic risks inherent in operating in the sector concerned" would be substantial.

[E]   Article 235 as a Backdoor Route to Annulment

MERKUR-AUSSENHANDELS-GMBH v. COMMISSION
Case 43/72, [1973] ECR 1055

Note 1 (Both questions) — The ECJ had, in *Plaumann*, Case 25/62, [1963] ECR 108, taken the view that "an administrative measure which has not been annulled cannot of itself constitute a wrongful act on the part of the administration inflicting damages upon those whom it affects". *Merkur* clearly overrules this approach. Separate from this issue is the question whether the applicant would have had standing to sue for annulment (whether or not it actually did so). In *Holtz v. Willemsen* (above) it becomes clear that this also was not necessary. Article 288 claims clearly are considered to be autonomous. (There are nonetheless some contrary cases in staff matters; see e.g., *Schots-Kortner and ORS v. Council, Commission and Parliament*, Joined Cases 15–33 etc./73, [1974] ECR 177.)

Note 2 (Both questions) It follows from the ECJ's rulings requiring the serious breach of a superior rule of law to justify an award of damages that litigants may well fail in such claims while they might at the same time succeed in an Article 230 action (if they have standing and bring a timely claim). Clearly then the Court intended to preserve the autonomous nature of damages claims by applying different, or at least stricter criteria. An award of damages would not render the act illegal, but obviously it might be withdrawn or amended to avoid further claims.

[F] Joint Liability of the EU and a Member State

SA BIOVILAC NV v. EUROPEAN ECONOMIC COMMUNITY
Case 59/83, [1984] ECR 4057

Note 1 The Commission's argument arises out of the phenomenon already observed in Chapter 13, namely that EU legislation is largely *implemented* by the Member States. The broader issue therefore is the extent to which the Member States should be liable instead of the EU. In *Kampffmeyer v. Commission*, Joined Cases 5, 7, and 13–24/66, [1967] ECR 245, the ECJ refused to determine the damages until proceedings had been completed in the German courts.

There is a long line of authority suggesting that a remedy must first be shown to be possible in the national courts, beginning with *Haegeman v. Commission*, Case 96/71, [1972] ECR 1055. But suppose the Court cannot know for sure whether a remedy is available in the national courts? See T. Hartley in [1976] 1 EL Rev. 299–304, 396–399. There would also be discrepancies in the availability of national remedies.

See also *Dietz v. Commission*, Case 126/76, [1977] ECR 2431; *Krohn v. Commission*, Case 175/84, 1987 ECJ CELEX LEXIS 18 [1986] ECR 753; *Societe des Grands Moulins des Antilles v. Commission*, 99/74, [1975] ECR 1531; *Lesieur Cotelle S.A. v. Commission*, Joined Cases 67–85/75, [1976] ECR 391.

Chapter 15

EU LAW IN NATIONAL COURTS

§ 15.02 THE ARTICLE 234 REFERRAL

[A] Requirement for a Genuine Case or Controversy?

FOGLIA v. NOVELLO
Case 104/79, [1980] ECR 745

Note 1 (Both questions) — As the Court emphasized in the second judgment, it is the duty of the national court to explain fully why an ECJ ruling is necessary. In the first case this had not been made clear so the ECJ took its own view, which was that there was no genuine dispute between the parties who were thus, through the national court, using the Article 234 procedure to obtain a purely advisory opinion. In the second judgment, the ECJ accepted that there might be a sufficient reason for the national court to require an opinion, but reserved to itself the ultimate right to decline jurisdiction. In this case the Italian proceeding could be viewed as merely a device for bringing into question the laws of another Member State, or for settling a question of interpretation of a contract where the parties were not in dispute. If that is indeed the primary purpose of the litigants' actions, the ECJ would not accept jurisdiction. The Court's view clearly was that it would not decide purely hypothetical issues nor would it allow itself to become a resource of legal opinions. In that sense it was clearly very concerned to establish a genuine case or controversy.

As is evident from its statement in *Mangold*, the ECJ's concern primarily is that its judgment must be necessary to resolve a national court case — thus it does reserve the right to decline a reference where there is no connection whatsoever.

[B] Ripeness

PRETORE DI SALO v. PERSONS UNKNOWN
Case 14/86, 1987 ECJ CELEX LEXIS 357, [1987] ECR 2545

Note 1 (All questions) — This case usually is considered to touch on the question of whether or not the institution referring the case qualifies as a *court* envisaged by Article 234. However, the absence of a judicial proceeding in the conventional sense also raises questions around the existence of any case or controversy at the point in the inquiry at which the reference is made. This is accentuated by the ECJ's ruling that a second reference on the same points could subsequently be made once the defendants were identified. On the other hand, it might be necessary to answer the questions at this stage in order to determine whether under the Italian implementing law, there was any cause of action. This was a matter for the national court, but the ECJ did confirm that the directive itself could not create any criminal obligations (see the materials on this subject in chapter 3).

[C] Litigation Involving the Compatibility of the Laws of Another Member State with EU Law

FOGLIA v. NOVELLO (No. 2)
Case 244/80, [1981] ECR 3045

Note 1 The Court did *not* say that it would not rule on questions relating to the laws of another Member State. However, its approach on the case or controversy issue was the response to its admonition that special care needed to be taken where such issues arose to safeguard against the possibility of abuse of the Article 234 procedure. In essence, it looked like the parties were simply trying to use the procedure to obtain an opinion for a contrived lawsuit.

As to the question of bring the laws of one state into question in the courts of another, there are interesting analogies with early U.S. law. One of the earliest cases under the new constitution involved proceedings brought by a resident of one state against another state in the courts of the United States, *Chisholm v. Georgia*, 2 U.S. (2 Dall.) 419, 1 L.Ed. 440 (1793). The result was the 11th Amendment, prohibiting such actions. (The state of Georgia had actually threatened to hang anyone seeking to execute the court's judgment.)

It is noteworthy that while the Eleventh Amendment prohibits federal courts from exercising jurisdiction over state governments in certain circumstances, it does not bar state courts from asserting jurisdiction over their own state government or over the government of another state.

Note 2 International law might be a determinant in the decision by the state court to make a ruling on French law. That is not an EU law issue however, according the Court. (This may be rather outdated. Consider for example the obligations of article 10 as developed by the Court and note that the Court referenced the then current state of EU law.)

Note 3 The national court was left without a ruling on the Article 90 question. It might therefore either decide for itself or refuse to give the declaratory judgment

Note 4 (All questions) — On the whole this is a very unusual circumstance. There is no evidence that the Court would decline to give a ruling wherever a genuine case existed. As a practical matter, such cases seem to be quite rare. However, it is now clear that the Court is not concerned with this issue. This is viewed as entirely an issue for the State court. The government of the State concerned is of course able to submit its own position in article 234 proceedings.

Note 6 The *Sfakianakis* decision did not require the Greek court to uphold a ruling related to Greek law, but merely to respect the ruling of the Hungarian court. This case therefore is quite narrow in its implications. However, the broader issue would be what position to take if the Hungarian court had made a determination about Greek law. Probably the Court would want to hear such a case in order to provide an interpretation of EU law, and then it would be up to the Greek court to apply it, based on its own understanding of the ruling.

[D]   References in Arbitration Proceedings

NORDSEE DEUTSCHE HOCHSEEFISCHEREI GMBH v. REEDEREI MOND HOCHSEEFISCHEREI NORDSTERN AG & CO. KG AND REEDEREI FRIEDRICH BUSSE HOCHSEEFISCHEREI NORDSTERN AG & CO. KG
Case 102/81, [1982] ECR 1095

Note 1 Q1 — Since in this case the parties were free to choose the ordinary courts, the ECJ would not accept jurisdiction.

Q2 — The Court accepts that references from an arbitrator may be justiciable where the law gave the parties no choice but to arbitrate. Where, however, a dispute is before the regular courts, the parties cannot prevent a reference, because this is a decision for the court, and the court is empowered by overriding EU law (Article 234).

Note 2 (All questions) — The strictly legal logic behind refusals to hear references from "voluntary" institutions lies in Article 234 itself: the "court" must be "of a Member State". Arbitrations by their nature, particularly international arbitrations, may take place wherever the parties have stipulated both the choice of law and venue are in the hands of the parties. In those circumstances it is hard to see how the mere "chance" that an arbitration takes place in a Member State can qualify it as a court of that Member State.

From a broader policy standpoint, a case can be made for including arbitrations particularly where these are the prevalent method of dispute resolution (e.g., shipping matters). There is a risk of significantly divergent views of EU law being taken by arbitrators.

Note 3 Q1 — The ECJ should accept jurisdiction in the event of a reference. If in the course of determining an issue of national law a court in a Member State decides that it needs guidance on a point of EU law, it should be permitted to make a reference to the ECJ under Article 234, especially since EU law is directly applicable and (often) directly effective in the legal systems of the Member States.

Q2 — If the parties to a contract choose New York law as the law governing their contract, it would include U.S. federal law insofar as it might affect the contract. Under Article VI of the Constitution, applicable federal law (i.e., the Constitution, treaties and federal statutes) would be supreme over any conflicting state law and should therefore be applied to issues arising under the contract.

[E] "Acte Clair"

CILFIT v. MINISTRY OF HEALTH
Case 283/81, [1982] ECR 3415

Note 1 Q1 — It is not unreasonable to conclude from the limitations described by the ECJ that it does not favor the *acte clair* doctrine. For example, almost every case is likely to raise the issue as to whether the EU law or Treaty provision has in fact a consistent meaning in all languages. How is a national court able to determine that on its own?

Q2 — The ECJ seems a little more comfortable where the decision not to refer is made based on prior identical questions having already been answered. On the other hand, an issue of first impression would surely require a reference.

Perhaps as its caseload increases the Court may no longer be so anxious to ensure references are made in cases where the matter seems already to have been decided or is relatively clear in the language of the jurisdiction where it arises.

Note 2 The problem does not really lie with the *acte clair* doctrine as such but with the degree of willingness of courts to make references. There is often a reluctance for courts below the final recourse level to make references because of the delay in legal process and the costs. Consider the cases set out in sections (2) and (3) of the chapter — there could be damages claim here, or a requirement for the availability of a procedure to challenge the refusal.

Note 3 Again, referencing the *Van Schijndel* decision, it is evident that differences in the remedies and procedures available in the various Member States will have an impact on the effectiveness of Article 234. The Court will continue to look to Article 10 and the duty of sincere cooperation to overcome these divergences.

Note 4 There is no reason why state constitutional law would not apply — a due process requirement for example — at least if it reinforces EU rights.

Q2 — Yes

Q3 — Yes, in circumstances where the issue could be raised in more than one Member State.

Q4 — This is inherent in the EU structure.

[F] Consequences of a Judgment Declaring that National Law is Incompatible with EU Law

OFFICE NATIONAL DES PENSIONS v. EMILIENNE JONKMAN AND HELENE VERCHEVAL AND NOELLE PERMESAEN v.OFFICE NATIONAL DES PENSIONS
Joined cases C-231/06 to C-233/06, 2007 ECJ CELEX LEXIS 349, [2007] ECR I-NYR

Note 1 The action required would not be contradictory since the ECJ has no power to "strike down" national law. However, any injured party might have a damages claim for the period that the infringing law remains in effect.

[G] References Relating to the Areas Covered by the TEU

GESTORES PRO AMNISTIA, JUAN MARI OLANO OLANO AND JULENZELARAIN ERRASTI v. COUNCIL
Case C-354/04 P, [2006] ECJ CELEX LEXIS 619

Note 1 The Court's reasoning is quite fascinating. It examines the notion of a common position and makes the assumption that such actions were not intended to have legal effects for third parties. It then concludes that it would have jurisdiction to determine whether the act did have such an effect. If it did, then it would have been improperly adopted as a common position.

§ 15.03 JUDICIAL REVIEW OF EU ACTS IN THE COURTS OF THE MEMBER STATES

FIRMA FOTO-FROST v. HAUPTZOLLAMT LUEBECK-OST
Case 314/85, 1987 ECJ CELEX LEXIS 200, [1987] ECR 4199

Note 1 Unlike the U.S. Supreme Court, the ECJ has a right to the last word on validity only if the issue is referred to it. By contrast, through the certiorari process, the United States Supreme Court always has the authority to review on appeal a ruling of a state court on the constitutionality of a treaty or a federal statute.

Note 2 (All questions) — The Court was only concerned about invalidity and saw no threat to the legal order of the EU from a state court decision to *uphold* EU legislation. In this regard, there was unlikely to arise any inconsistency with an ECJ ruling, because by the time the national decision has been handed down, in all likelihood, the opportunity to challenge a measure under Article 230 will have passed. Second, in purely national proceedings, the EU authorities have no right to intervene to defend the act. Third, there is a need to ensure uniformity of approach. For an English case see, *Regina v. Searle* (Court of Appeals), [1995] 3 CMLR 196.

Note 3 (All questions) — It is plain that the conditions laid down by the ECJ for permitting national courts to take interim measures are designed to ensure that the ECJ eventually gets to rule on the final validity or invalidity of the EU measure. Therefore, these conditions are designed to ensure uniformity of approach. See further *Atlanta Fruchthandelsgesellschaft MbH v. Bundesamt für Ernährung und Forstwirtschaft*, Case C-465/93, 1995 ECJ CELEX LEXIS 242, [1995] ECR I-3761.

TWD TEXTILWERKE DEGGENDORF GMBH v. GERMANY
Case 188/92, 1994 ECJ CELEX LEXIS 113, [1994] ECR I-833

Note 1 Q1/2 — This decision is restricted to those cases where the party challenging the EU measure could have brought an action for annulment under Article 230. The problem for individual litigants is to know when such annulment actions are possible. It is clear from chapter 14 that the cases are far from definitive — see e.g., the *Kwekerij*

Gebroeders case where some litigants were found to have no standing (and the Court recognized then that they should be able to challenge under Article 234) while the Landbouwschap itself was found to have standing. This could create difficulties for the national courts.

Q3 — This itself would require reference under Article 234.

Note 3 In TWD the ECJ expressly acknowledged its earlier ruling in *Rau v. BALM* that it was possible for proceedings to be conducted both in the ECJ under article 230 and in the national courts under Article 234. The *Rau* case preceded the establishment of the CFI so the problem did not arise.

§ 15.04 DUTY TO ENSURE THE EFFECTIVENESS OF EU LAW

[A] The General Principles Equivalence to National Protection

UNIBET (LONDON) LTD AND UNIBET (INTERNATIONAL) LTD v. JUSTITIEKANSLERN
Case C-432/05, 2007 ECJ CELEX LEXIS 153, [2007] ECR ___

Note 1 First, as regards procedures, the overall principle is that national law must in some manner permit the proper assertion of EU law. Thus in an extreme case where this was completely impossible, the national courts would have to create a procedure to allow that (para 41). However, this would be a very unusual circumstance. Normally there would be some avenue for doing so, and in that case, the national courts are required only to accord parties asserting EU law claims the same protection as they would have for national claims. Thus the Court is expressly rejecting the notion that there could be a requirement for some kind of uniform EU procedure in all Member States. Next the Court confirmed that interim relief must be possible (per *Factortame*) but this is not necessary where the underlying claim itself is inadmissible (as here, due to the absence of a right to bring a free standing action for judicial review). Third, where there is no procedure for admitting the main action, there is no requirement to suspend the application of national law unless this is also permitted for purely national disputes.

[B] National Courts' Obligations to Raise EU Law Issues

OCEANO GRUPO EDITORIAL SA v. ROCIO MURCIANO QUINTERO), AND SALVAT EDITORES SA v. JOSE M. SANCHEZ ALCON PRADES JOSE LUIS COPANO BADILLO AND OTHERS
Joined cases C-240/98 to C-244/98, 2000 ECJ CELEX LEXIS 308, [2000] ECR I-4941

Note 1 First, there is a substantial difference between the facts here and the issue in *Van Schijndel*. In that case, there was a practical impossibility of raising an issue of EU competition law in the absence of any evidence or other factual basis for doing so. To insist that the national court raise it would be tantamount to requiring it to introduce a new cause of action into the proceedings. Admittedly, one might argue that to enforce a contract that is blatantly anticompetitive would be against public policy and the Court might have to take cognizance of that situation under its domestic law. However, this was certainly not obvious in *Van Schijndel*.

By contrast, in the *Oceano* case, the national court was faced with a situation that had already been addressed several times by the Spanish Supreme Court. The question did not require the production of any evidence or the assertion of a civil claim. It was in a sense just a question of the Court's determining it own jurisdiction. This was something entirely within its power to do and not to have raised the issue would then itself have been a breach of EU law.

[C] Enforcement of EU Rights

THERESA EMMOTT v. MINISTER FOR SOCIAL WELFARE AND ATTORNEY GENERAL
Case C-208/90, 1991 ECJ CELEX LEXIS 424, [1991] ECR I-4269

Note 1 (Both questions) — Some have taken the position that this case should be confined to its facts. It focuses only on the period prior to implementation of a directive and ensures that a person is not prejudiced in asserting rights where she was not yet in a position to know what her rights actually were. One could argue however that the same situation could as a practical matter exist after the implementation of the directive. The particular nature of a directive is that it is not directly applicable (although creating direct effects) so it is not obvious to what extent it actually would create rights for individuals. To allow a Member State to disbar an action because of its own failure to observe its obligations would be seriously to impair the effectiveness of EU law.

[D] Recovery of Improper Charges

AMMINISTRAZIONE DELLE FINANZE DELLO STATO v. SPA SAN GIORGIO
Case 199/82, [1983] ECR 3595

Note 1 EU law does seem to be privileged in this particular situation. In dealing with claims for recovery of charges that were impermissible under EU law, the Court implicitly is taking the view that the practice of throwing up evidentiary obstacles to claims against the State, whether national or EU based, is not a satisfactory or objectively justifiable practice in any event, and as such, should certainly not impede the assertion of an EU right. If that is indeed the Court's view, this could lead to some interesting situations where the Court is effectively evaluating the purpose of national, albeit non-discriminatory, rules.

§ 15.05 ACTIONS AGAINST MEMBER STATES FOR COMPENSATION FOR BREACH OF EU LAW

[A] The Elements of the Claim

FRANCOVICH v. ITALY
Joined Cases 6 & 9/90, 1991 ECJ CELEX LEXIS 369, [1991] ECR I-5357

Note 1 The Court reverted to the language it had originally used in *Costa v. ENEL.* The Treaties create rights for individuals. Where they cannot invoke the directive itself, they should at least have the ability to recover damages for loss occasioned by a Member State's breach in failing to transpose a directive into national law. (As will be seen in the *Factortame* case below, this principle now also applies even where rights can be invoked.)

Note 2 (All questions) — The question that this decision begs is: what are the conditions under which compensation would be due? As later cases indicate, the Court has analogised such cases to the Article 235/288 action, although this is far from solving the question. In principle an action against the government would be possible — the biggest issue would be to calculate some form of damages for actual loss. This was much the situation in *Johnston*, (see chapter 17, *infra*), where the evidential rule that a government minister's certificate was conclusive as to whether a matter was to be considered one of national security was found to conflict with the provisions of Directive 76/207. This directive contemplated at least a right to independent judicial review of such a certificate. The national rule was found to be a violation of the directive and the national courts were required by Article 10 of the EC Treaty to ensure that the national rule complied with the directive. There are now a number of cases, resulting from sex discrimination proceedings, where national rules have been found to interfere with the full intent of EU legislation.

BRASSERIE DU PECHEUR SA v. BUNDESREPUBLIK DEUTSCHLAND AND THE QUEEN v. SECRETARY OF STATE FOR TRANSPORT, EX PARTE: FACTORTAME LTD AND OTHERS
Joined Cases C-46/93 and C-48/93, 1996 ECJ CELEX LEXIS 589, [1996] ECR I-1029

Note 1 In the first place, the Court explicitly held that claims for reparations may also be made even if the individual had the right to invoke the EU law against application of the national law (direct effect). Second, it adopted a different reasoning based this time on articles 235/288 and the parallel right at the EU level to seek damages for breach against EU institutions.

Note 2 This approach indicates that there is one system, with uniform principles. Yet the procedures of the Member States may not allow for this. This could then entail the explicit creation of a new form of procedure. Perhaps the real challenge lies in applying the criteria that the ECJ has developed for article 235/288 claims. The solution of course is that the national courts should always refer such questions to the ECJ.

Note 3 The Court addressed this issue in the same way that it has done in the context of ensuring the effectiveness of EU law — see the *Unibet* case, above. While in principle parties should have at least equivalent protection to that afforded for claims relating to national laws or acts, there may be a point at which this no longer is sufficient — the Court cites for example the English rule on misfeasance of Government officers, which grounds such claims under English law, while there is no means for bringing an action against Parliament for enacting non-conforming legislation. Thus new and unique procedures for EU claims are required in such cases.

[B]   Discretionary and Non-Discretionary Acts or Omissions

WALTER RECHBERGER, RENATE GREINDL, HERMANN HOFMEISTER AND OTHERS v. AUSTRIA
Case C-140/97, 1999 ECJ CELEX LEXIS 256, [1999] ECR I-3499

Note 1 (All questions) — The Court takes the view that a failure to transpose a directive in any respect where no discretion is granted — such as the deadline for transposition — is always going to be a sufficiently serious breach.

Note 2 (All questions) — It is hard to imagine how the Court could give much more precision given the nature of its rule. It is essentially indicating that it is a matter of factual evidence.

[C]   Damages and Fault

BRASSERIE DU PECHEUR SA v. BUNDESREPUBLIK DEUTSCHLAND AND THE QUEEN v. SECRETARY OF STATE FOR TRANSPORT, EX PARTE: FACTORTAME LTD AND OTHERS
Joined Cases C-46/93 and C-48/93, 1996 ECJ CELEX LEXIS 589 [1996] ECR I-1029

Note 1 The Court is at pains to establish an EU standard for both damages and fault. The former is based strictly on providing adequate compensation for the loss suffered, taking into account any mitigating actions open to the plaintiffs. So far as fault is concerned, there is no such requirement as such, at least in terms of intentional or negligence factors. Instead the Court focuses on the "sufficiently serious" breach.

Note that the Court sets a separate and additional condition — that the damages and other remedies must not be less than comparable remedies for breaches of national law. This then serves not only as a general rule as to the nature of the remedy but also as a minimum standard.

[D] Who is Responsible?

SALOMONE HAIM v. KASSENARZTLICHE VEREINIGUNG NORDRHEIN
Case C-424/97, 2000 ECJ CELEX LEXIS 103, [2000] ECR I-5123

Note 1 It would appear from the Court's judgment that it is somewhat indifferent as to the source of the damages, although making it clear that they must be due from a "public law body." Thus, it would presumably be unacceptable that the State might seek to impose an obligation on private interests to make good the loss as this would entirely defeat the underlying purpose of the action.

GERHARD KÖBLER v. AUSTRIA
Case C-224/01, 2003 ECJ CELEX LEXIS 403, [2003] ECR I-10239

Note 1 The Court drew a clear distinction between the decision on the original claim and the subsequent claim for damages arising from the first judgment. This is not actually an easy distinction, since effectively the award of damages would necessarily bring into question the compliance of the Court with EU law.

Note 2 The Court alluded to the responsibility of the State acting through the court system. This is a well understood concept in international law.

Note 3 The implication in this question is that a court of final resort that failed to make a reference would expose the State to liability in damages. However, it is far from clear that this would satisfy the causation requirement since it would not necessarily be known whether as a result of obtaining a ruling, the national court would have come to a different conclusion.

Note 4 This issue is alluded to in the Court's judgment. It is hard to imagine any judge wanting to take on such an issue, so there would probably be an attempt to refer the matter to the highest court.

§ 15.06 ACTIONS FOR DAMAGES AGAINST PRIVATE INDIVIDUALS BASED ON A BREACH OF EU LAW

COURAGE LTD v. BERNARD CREHAN AND BERNARD CREHAN v. COURAGE LTD AND OTHERS
Case C-453/99, 2001 ECJ CELEX LEXIS 755, [2001] ECR I-6297

Note 1 The Court indirectly affirms that some form of action must be available since the national courts have the duty to ensure that EU rights are upheld, and a right to be compensated for loss arising from a breach of EU law by another private individual is part of the protection.

Note 2 As a general principle, the common law of contract does not recognize a difference in bargaining power, compared with civil law systems that place heavy duties on parties who impose terms on consumers — so-called *contrats d'adhésion*. This factor should be taken into account in assessing an overall level of fault.

VINCENZO MANFREDI v. LLOYD ADRIATICO ASSICURAZIONI SPA, ANTONIO CANNITO v. FONDIARIA SAI SPA AND NICOLO TRICARICO AND PASQUALINA MURGOLO v. ASSITALIA SPA
Joined Cases C-295/04 to C-298/04, 2006 ECJ CELEX LEXIS 348, [2006] ECR I-6619

Note 1 (All questions) — Obviously there are many questions to be answered here. As class actions build for violations of Article 81, as they exist perhaps to some extent in the U.S., it is to be expected that the Court will lay down some EU standards. For example, that the forum chosen for an action bears some reasonable connection to the acts complained of, and that damages should be designed to compensate for loss (whatever this actually is in an antitrust civil action) with a caveat that the remedies should be no less favorable than under national law.

Note 2 Yes, the ECJ is not going to rewrite national contract law.

§ 15.07 COOPERATION BETWEEN STATE COURTS AND EU INSTITUTIONS

COMMISSION NOTICE ON THE COOPERATION BETWEEN THE COMMISSION AND THE COURTS OF THE EU MEMBER STATES IN THE APPLICATION OF ARTICLES 81 AND 82
[2004] OJ C 101/04

Note 2 The introduction of civil claims procedures might help or hinder the leniency program. If parties are afraid that coming forward will increase their risk of suit, they might hesitate. On the other hand, by coming in first they could have the opportunity to settle the suits before other parties have prepared themselves. Parties seem to have accommodated this issue in the U.S..

Part V
FUNDAMENTAL RIGHTS

Chapter 16

THE EU FRAMEWORK OF FUNDAMENTAL RIGHTS

§ 16.02 THE ECHR AND THE CHARTER OF FUNDAMENTAL RIGHTS

Note 1 As indicated in the introduction to the chapter, the Charter represents an attempt to bring together basic freedoms, social rights and economic rights. As such it goes well beyond the scope of the US Bill of Rights. However, the table below suggests at least a rough correlation between some Charter provisions and the Bill of Rights.

Charter Article	U.S. Constitution Amendment
2.1 Prohibition of the death penalty	VIII cruel and unusual punishment (?)
4 Torture and inhumane treatment	VIII cruel and unusual punishment
5 Prohibition of Slavery	XV Voting rights. Also V/XIV regarding due process, though not extending to Member States in the case of the EU except when implementing EU law XIII prohibiting slavery
6 Liberty and security	IV warrants and V due process
10 Freedom of thought, conscience And religion	I Church and state/free speech and assembly
11 Freedom of expression	I Freedom of speech
12 Freedom of assembly	I Freedom of Assembly
16 Freedom to conduct a business	XIV as regards citizenship rights
17 Right to Property	V Due Process
21/23 Equality/non discrimination	V and XIV Due process
47 Right to fair trial	V due process
48 Presumption of innocence	V due process
49 Proportionality	V due process and VIII cruel and unusual punishment
50 Double jeopardy	V due process

Note 2 The Charter imitates the ECHR in this regard. Some statements (such as 2.1) may be regarded as principles that influence interpretation of other provisions and various balancing factors while others are capable of specific application to particular situations (such as 2.2).

Note 3 Many of the Charter provisions could be regarded as contradictory somewhere along the trajectory of their respective meanings. As indicated in Note 2, some of the more principle-type provisions may actually be invoked to limit the scope of other rights when used in the context of balancing society needs against the needs of individuals. This will become evident from cases such as *Omega*.

§ 16.03   THE REACH OF EU FUNDAMENTAL RIGHTS

[A]   Effects on Member States

JOHNSTON   v.   CHIEF   CONSTABLE   OF   THE   ROYAL   ULSTER CONSTABULARY
Case 222/84, 1986 ECJ CELEX LEXIS 103, [1986] ECR 1651

Note 1 If an evidentiary procedure becomes subject to EU standards, it is hard to see why it would not then have an influence on how that rule might be applied in other circumstances including purely national law issues, on the principle that once it has been declared unacceptable for EU purposes, it is harder to justify it for other purposes.

Note 2 (All questions) — If former Directive 64/221 could be considered as fulfilling the requirement of a fair hearing, this is equivalent to a direct application of the ECHR substantive requirements to national law through EU legislation. One must certainly wonder whether that is what the Council meant to do, but in any event, what has happened here is quite fundamental. After all, in any country where the ECHR does not apply directly to national law, there is an elaborate process for triggering review in Strasbourg, including a requirement to satisfy national procedures first. So the ability to assert ECHR rights in opposition to national law through an EU connection is quite subversive of that structure.

ELLINIKI RADIOFONIA TILEORASSI ANONIMI ETAIRIA (ERT AE) AND ANOTHER   v.   DIMOTIKI   ETAIRIA   PLIROFORISSIS   AND   SOTIRIOS KOUVELAS AND ANOTHER
Case C-260/89, 1991 ECJ CELEX LEXIS 179, [1991] ECR I-2925

Note 1 EU fundamental rights must be applied in any case where a Member State is invoking one of the EU recognized exceptions to free movement, here manifested in article 55 EC. The ECJ did not give any direction to the national court as to how the balancing of public policy vs. freedom of expression should be carried out. There was thus a potential for further references although this did not occur. The ECJ actually seems to be distorting the intent of the ECHR here. The latter speaks of judging public policy exceptions to the freedom of expression, while in the *ERT* decision, the question was whether public policy grounds could justify an exception to the freedom to provide services between Member States. This seems to imply that the latter freedom embodies the freedom of expression, but this was not how the court approached it, and indeed the economic freedoms ought perhaps to be considered as standalone and not importing the ECHR freedoms as part of their content.

WERNER MANGOLD v. RUDIGER HELM
Case C-144/04, 2005 ECJ CELEX LEXIS 607, [2005] ECR I-9981

Note 2 Mr Mangold had of course no right to invoke the directive against another private employer, but the Court relied instead on a breach of his fundamental rights by the German government in the application of EU legislation, notwithstanding that the deadline for implementation of 2000/78 had not yet passed; he might have had an argument if the law as amended by Germany had been adopted as the state's transposition measure (based on the duty of the state not to take measures before the deadline for transposition had arrived that were actually contrary to the directive — see the *Inter-environnement* case in chapter 3) but this was not the case here. Also, the earlier directive, 1999/70 although in force, was not helpful since it did not expressly address these issues; Mr Mangold did not claim that Germany was in breach of this directive, which moreover, given the ECJ's approach, might itself have been called into question to the extent that it could be interpreted as impliedly permitting age discrimination as one of the objectively justifiable factors. Instead, the Court relied on the general statements in the earlier framework directive regarding the EU approach to discrimination on all kinds, coupled with the three year special delay in implementing the directive that had been approved for Germany (see para 73).

All in all, this case seems to strain the argument that EU fundamental rights only apply to Member States when implementing EU legislation. One may wonder about the implications. Could this lead to a much more generalized application of the Charter once it becomes part of EU law on a par with the Treaties? Could any action by a Member State within any area where the EC Treaty has some relevance then become subject to appraisal under the Charter?

Note 3 One might be able to distinguish the *Sweden* and *Grant* cases on the basis that they had to do with social security or private benefits, and the laws of the Member States were by no means consistent on the treatment of same sex partnerships with respect to benefits entitlement. However, it seems a little strained to make generalized observations about equality of treatment being part of the constitutional traditions of the Member States after denying equal treatment to persons based on their sexual orientation.

THE SOCIETY FOR THE PROTECTION OF UNBORN CHILDREN IRELAND LTD v. STEPHEN GROGAN AND OTHERS
Case C-159/90, 1991 ECJ CELEX LEXIS 409, [1991] ECR I-4685

Note 1 The essential consideration here was whether the defendants in the main action were actually engaging in any activity protected by the EC Treaty, namely availing themselves of any of the freedoms, particularly article 49. In fact the Court held they were not, rather they were asserting the right of free expression under the Irish Constitution. This contrasts with the *Schmidberger* case, following, where the assertion of free expression directly interfered with the exercise by others of their free movement rights.

[B] Effects on TEU and EC Treaties Themselves?

EUGEN SCHMIDBERGER, INTERNATIONALE TRANSPORTE UND PLANZUGE v. AUSTRIA
Case C-112/00, 2003 ECJ CELEX LEXIS 75, [2003] ECR I-5659

Note 1 One could evaluate the issue here in a number of ways. First, the state's action in permitting the demonstration as a manifestation of the freedom of expression, being part of national law, can be used as here to inhibit free movement of goods, and would require to be evaluated on a *Cassis* rationale; or, one could consider that the EU rule on free movement is itself subject to constraints insofar as it should not be applied to deny fundamental rights. The Court seems rather to follow the former path. It lays emphasis on the action of the Government rather than the underlying principle of freedom of expression, which then perhaps is not called into question. What is evaluated for an objective justification is the decision to allow the demonstration to proceed, and this was objectively justified and not disproportionate. However, one would need to make sure in such cases that the national authority did not step outside the bounds of a proportionate response. The conflict is not between a fundamental right and the free movement of goods as such, but rather the potential behavior of the Member State when permitting free expression to interfere with free movement.

Chapter 17

DUE PROCESS

§ 17.02 STANDARDS APPLICABLE TO LEGISLATIVE AND EXECUTIVE ACTION

[A] Proportionality

BOSPHORUS HAVA YOLLARI TURIZM VE TICARET AS v. MINISTER FOR TRANSPORT, ENERGY AND COMMUNICATIONS AND OTHERS
Case C-84/95,1996 ECJ CELEX LEXIS 489, [1996] ECR I-3953

LASERDISKEN APS v. KULTURMINISTERIET
C-479/04, 2006 ECJ CELEX LEXIS 447, [2006] ECR I-8089

ALROSA COMPANY LTD v. COMMISSION
Case T-170/06, 2007 ECJ CELEX LEXIS 449 [2007] ECR NYR

Note 1 (All questions) — The context of each of these cases is critical to understanding the application of the principle.

In *Bosphorus* the EU was carrying out UN policy. The imposition of sanctions against Yugoslavia involved a grave human rights situation which merited strong action. The measures adopted may have had unfortunate results for an individual company but were acceptable when balanced against the objectives. The Court seems to take the view that measures imposing economic sanctions are by their nature harsh and therefore may cause damage to all kinds of interests not the direct target of them. Proportionality therefore cannot be brought to bear once it is accepted that the sanctions themselves are legal. Bosphorus of course could be criticized for not having taken legal advice and extracted themselves from the lease arrangements. Moreover, the Yugoslav owner may have benefited from the fact that it did not have unused aircraft to store and maintain while the sanctions were in force. The measure is not therefore as harsh it might seem.

In *Laserdisken,* the question was of a quite different order. Here, the issue was whether the EU had exercised its legislative discretion in a balanced way. As already seen in Chapter 14, the EU Courts will generally not disturb the choice and are very reluctant to insert themselves into what are political or economic issues.

In *Alrosa*, the Court was examining an individual decision under the competition rules. Here, it is willing to investigate the entire factual circumstances of the decision to determine whether a remedy is proportionate to the conduct it seeks to prohibit. This is of course an administrative act, and justifies far more intensive judicial control.

[B] Non-Retroactivity/Legitimate Expectations/Legal Certainty

MARKS & SPENCER PLC v. COMMISSIONERS OF CUSTOMS & EXCISE
Case C-62/00, 2002 ECJ CELEX LEXIS 262, [2002] ECR I-6325

Note 1 (All Questions) — The principle of non-retroactivity is a manifestation of the general rule that actions by the administration cannot defeat a party's legitimate expectations as to how it is to be treated. It is therefore not an absolute principle but depends on whether a party has suffered financial loss because it took certain steps in reliance, legitimately, on the conduct and assurances of the administration. The Court accepted that imposing time limits which would preclude recoveries for the past after a certain point in time is not necessarily contrary to EU law, particularly if it furthers legal certainty.

[C] Discrimination/Unfair Burden

ROYAL SCHOLTEN-HONIG (HOLDINGS) LTD v. INTERVENTION BOARD FOR AGRICULTURAL PRODUCE; TUNNEL REFINERIES LTD v. INTERVENTION BOARD FOR AGRICULTURAL PRODUCE
Joined Cases 103 and 145/77, [1978] ECR 2037

Note 1 (All questions) — This case arose before the Charter had come into existence and in fact before the Court had started to refer to the ECHR as a source of fundamental rights. However, the type of equality referred to here is a manifestation of the "equality of burden" principle that derives from administrative law. No party should be required to bear an undue portion of the burden imposed by administrative regulation. It thus has a long history in the laws of the Member States and is brought into EU law as a result of the reference to "a rule of law relating to [the Treaty's] application" (article 234). The Court has rarely upheld such arguments. It is not clear that it was really doing so here either — but more specifically relying on the requirement of non-discrimination in article 40 EC. In any event, the primary concern was that the Council erred in not taking account of the true impact of the production levy on sugar producers as compared with the impact of the isoglucose producers who were in a comparable position.

§ 17.03 PROCEDURAL DUE PROCESS

[A] Timely Action

JCB SERVICE v. COMMISSION
Case T-67/01, 2004 ECJ CELEX LEXIS 20, [2004] ECR II-49

Note 1 (Both questions) — This case arose of course under the original Regulation 17 procedure where an agreement had to be notified in order to qualify for consideration for an exemption. The sheer volume of notifications made the Commission's job extremely difficult and it had resorted to issuing comfort letters which were not decisions and could not be challenged, hence did not need detailed reasoning. All of this was a highly unsatisfactory state of affairs and interfered with more important tasks including investigation of cartels. The abolition of the system was thus to be welcomed. This is probably not the only case where a notification took as long to receive a formal response. Given this background it is not surprising that the Court was not disposed to condemn the Commission for the 27 years it had taken in this case. However, from a policy point of view the Court was consistent with its approach regarding such matters. As already seen in chapter 13, it is concerned only to make sure that the rights of the defense are not prejudiced and in that regard noted that the Commission had not sought to rely in its SO on any ground that related to the matters the subject of its long delayed decision. The Court's purpose in basing its ruling on preservation of the rights of the defense is not primarily to see that justice is done but to ensure that the Commission has behaved in accordance with principles of sound administration. Although the rights of the defense might resemble some of the rights that appear under "Justice" for criminal matters, they cannot be equated. This is administrative law, not criminal law.

[B] Presumption of Innocence

JCB SERVICE v. COMMISSION
Case T-67/01, 2004 ECJ CELEX LEXIS 20, [2004] ECR II-49
(second extract)

Note 1 JCB's allegations relating to the breach of the "presumption of innocence" again do not look familiar to a criminal lawyer for the simple reason that the Commission is both investigator and decision maker in competition matters, these being essentially of an administrative nature. The bias that JCB alleges is focused on actions by the Commission as investigator, allegedly showing that it had already made up its mind and was manufacturing a case to suit its ends. But in fact, as investigator, it is perfectly entitled to carry out its activities and use whatever documents it likes, if obtained properly and interpreted correctly. The Court will only focus on the final decision to determine whether the Commission has correctly appraised the conduct in question.

[C] Right to a Fair Hearing

ORGANISATION DES MODJAHEDINES DU PEUPLE D'IRAN v. COUNCIL OF THE EUROPEAN UNION
Case T-228/02, [2006] ECR NYR

Note 1 The judgment is quite confusing on this issue. The Court certainly asserts that the national fact-finding procedure should be governed by EU principles but in the same paragraph refer to restrictions on the right to a fair hearing "legally justified in national law". It seems to be following in effect the ECHR methodology which defers to national security and policy considerations. But this is the EU, not the ECHR, and the Member States here are implementing EU law, so all of the criteria used to appraise restrictions ought to be EU-based.

The CFI clearly followed the well trodden path of defining its role as one of ensuring that the rights of the defense were preserved, principally in this case by insisting on the requirement of detailed reasoning to enable it to verify the decisions that had been reached. This would require providing the CFI if necessary with confidential information. Again the emphasis is on ensuring sound administration. However, it is evident that the plaintiffs though otherwise, no doubt seeing themselves as having been branded in some form as criminals as a result of the public decisions freezing their assets. The case thus is somewhat delicately poised between administrative and criminal contexts, and one wonders whether it would not be more appropriate to analogize the procedures here with criminal law. If the EU judges only get to review for proper procedure and not to oversee the underlying process, does this not undermine the EU's reputation as a leader in upholding fundamental rights?

[D] Access to Files

BPB INDUSTRIES PLC AND BRITISH GYPSUM LTD v. COMMISSION
Case C-310/93 P., 1995 ECJ CELEX LEXIS 189, [1995] ECR I-865

Note 1 The requirement is to disclose all documents to all defendants relating to the case except those covered by business confidentiality.

[E]   The Right Against Self-incrimination/Right to Silence

ORKEM SA (CDF CHIMIE SA) v. COMMISSION; SOLVAY & CIE v. COMMISSION
Joined Cases 374/87 and 27/88, 1989 ECJ CELEX LEXIS 176, [1989] ECR 231

Note 1 Michel apparently learned the reasons for the Commission's decision in the course of the court proceedings. It clearly would not be satisfactory for any party to have to start expensive proceedings to find out the reasons for a decision when by law he was entitled to know them — it seems in Orkem that the reasons were fully communicated by the Commission but not, technically, to the appropriate company. The ECJ, consistent with its general approach, was not prepared to allow a mere formality to vitiate a Commission action where no substantial detriment to the rights of the defense occurred.

Note 2 (All questions) — Once again, this is not a criminal proceeding. Moreover, the Commission's ability to find an infringement is highly dependent on its securing evidence from the infringers themselves. To allow the infringers to refuse to supply it would thus completely undermine the Commission's role. On the other hand, the Court accepted that Orkem should not required to confess by being obliged to answer questions that proceeded from an assumption of illegal conduct. Thus, for example, to ask a party to give the date when a price fixing conspiracy began is not acceptable. But to ask a party whether it met other parties on a given date would be acceptable. Essentially, one could conclude that this is not because it is unjust to require someone to incriminate themselves, but that the goal of proper administration is not served by asking self-serving questions that force a party to admit to something that they deny. The purpose of the investigation is to obtain the facts, and obtaining a legal conclusion before the facts are collected is not going to enhance the chances of a decision's being upheld.

Note 3 The issue of self incrimination has become much more pointed since the inception of the leniency policy, because this encourages companies to produce evidence that inculpates them in illegal activity. If they have US exposure for the same conduct, such documents could end up in the hands of the DOJ or of private plaintiffs seeking triple damages. The practice is therefore to produce documents but provide only verbal descriptions of activities. This renders whatever record the Commission takes as hearsay and unusable in the US.

Note 4 (All questions) — The result of the Court's decision was only that Orkem did not have to respond to some of the Commission's questions. Hence this was only a step along the way to procuring an eventually sound decision.

§ 17.04   CRIMINAL JUSTICE

[A]   Right to a Fair Trial and and Effective Remedy

CRIMINAL PROCEEDINGS AGAINST MARIA PUPINO
Case C-105/03, 2005 ECJ CELEX LEXIS 774, [2005] ECR I-5285

Note 1 Although the Framework Decision is not invocable, failure of the national court to follow the interpretation of the ECJ in and of itself would be breach of the state's obligations under the TEU. However, if the court accepts the interpretation and then concludes that national law is incompatible, it is not authorized, at least by Union law, to disapply the national statute.

Note 2 The Court's interpretation of the Framework Decision included an evaluation of its consistency with fundamental rights, including of course the ECHR. The appraisal of this question was left to the national court, which is thus obliged in effect to take account of the ECHR at least so far as the application of the Framework Decision is concerned, as part of its national process, even if normally it the ECHR would only be relevant in an appeal to the Court of Human Rights after all national remedies are exhausted.

[B] Double Jeopardy

CRIMINAL PROCEEDINGS AGAINST LEOPOLD HENRI VAN ESBROECK
Case C-436/04, 2006 ECJ CELEX LEXIS 576, [2006] ECR I-2333

Note 1 Generally the Court's approach seems right, but there could be complications where the procedures followed in the other state are at odds with how the second state would view the offence and what action it would take. For example, in the case of a plea bargain resulting in a lighter sentence for a lesser charge, the second state might consider this to be totally unacceptable

Chapter 18
EU CITIZENSHIP RIGHTS

§ 18.02 RIGHTS OF ENTRY AND RESIDENCE

[A] Registration and Similar Requirements

LYNNE WATSON AND ALLESSANDRO BELMANN
Case 118/75 [1976] ECR 1185

Note 1 The Court's approach is to focus on the effects of the national legislation — whomever it might affect — insofar as it might indirectly restrict free movement. It is perhaps difficult to see how the legislation in this case, as it applied to the Italian national, could really have had such an effect (although perhaps his incarceration for 6 months would have caused the British national to leave the country).

Note 2 The discrimination would not arise, in the Court's view, from the legitimate exercise of state power to monitor the presence of foreign nationals. The discrimination arises rather from the particularly harsh penalties that attached to violations of the reporting requirements.

A considerable body of jurisprudence has developed on the extent of the state's right to require residence permits, reporting obligations and so on (within the context of the secondary legislation, particularly Directive 68/360). See e.g., *Sagulo, Brenca, and Bakhouche*, Case 8/77, [1977] ECR 1495; *Royer*, Case 48/75, [1976] ECR 497.

Articles 14(2) and 18 do not seem to affect this situation in the present stage of development of EU law. See also *Regina v. Sec. Of State for the Home Dept. ex p. Vittorio Vitale*, [1995] 3 CMLR 605 (English High Court). Directive 2004/38 seems to endorse the continuation of registration requirements though residence permits are forbidden. However, it may well be that increased cooperation between Member States will essentially render such requirements obsolete.

[B] Restrictions Imposed by Private Organizations

UNION ROYALE BELGE DES SOCIETES DE FOOTBALL ASSOCIATION ASBL AND OTHERS v. JEAN-MARC BOSMAN
Case C-415/93, 1995 ECJ CELEX LEXIS 220, [1995] ECR I-4921

Note 1 This is a very difficult concept to understand, particularly now that article 39 has been extended also to private employers (per *Angonese*, as noted). Would they need to be acting under some form of government requirement related to a Treaty exception, or could they make up their own rules?

Note 2 One of the most interesting features of *Bosman* is that the rules applied to clubs, not individuals. This was a form of anticompetitive behavior but had been condoned by the Commission, action that the ECJ condemned.

[C]   Indirect Obstacles to Free Movement and Wholly Internal Situations

UNION ROYALE BELGE DES SOCIETES DE FOOTBALL ASSOCIATION ASBL AND OTHERS v. JEAN-MARC BOSMAN
Case C-415/93, 1995 ECJ CELEX LEXIS 220, [1995] ECR I-4921

Note 1 The ECJ took the view that it did not matter that the rules of the Association might apply predominantly to transfers and moves between clubs situated in the same Member State. Since it would not make sense to have a more liberal system for interstate transfers than for intrastate, the rule as a whole had to be found contrary to article 39. This might be compared with the *Lawyers Services* and *Klopp* cases in Chapter 7, *supra*, where the Court only declared the offending rules to be contrary to EU law to the extent that they were applied to out -of- state lawyers.

VOLKER GRAF v. FILZMOSER MASCHINENBAU GMBH
Case C-190/98, 2000 ECJ CELEX LEXIS 286, [2000] ECR I-493

Note 1 In general, following the *Bosman* ruling the Court has been willing to apply article 39 to rules that impose a burden on an individual who wishes to go to work in another Member State, even if by and large those rules normally affect intrastate situations. This seems somewhat of a departure from the more standard objective evaluation test seen elsewhere in the free movement provisions of the EC Treaty. The Court has indeed focused on a different test: does the state rule affect access to the labor market? It found in this case that it did not. Note that the German nationality of Mr Graf had nothing to do with the Court's reasoning, which is not based on discrimination.

MOSER v. LAND BADEN WURTTEMBERG
Case 180/83 [1984] ECR 3723

Note 1 (All questions) — The complainant argued that the restriction on his teaching rights in Germany would affect his job prospects in other EU countries. There was no suggestion, however, that this had happened, and the Court refused to entertain a purely hypothetical effect. Even if there were a proven detriment, it seems that the matter should still have been considered as entirely an internal German concern. This approach reflects one of the major problems in viewing the EC Treaty as a form of "constitution". It grants rights only in connection with interstate movement but leaves nationals at the mercy of their own governments. This distinction nonetheless could be broken down if the Court were to adopt a more rigorous approach in light of Article 18, which could be used to expand the Treaty's scope to cover internal matters through a more general connection with free movement (See the *Adams* case in Chapter 16). For a case found by the Court to be outside the scope of application of the EC Treaty, see *Friedrich Kremzow v. Austria*, Case C-299/95, 1997 ECJ CELEX LEXIS 286,[1997] ECR I-2629.

One might actually question whether in this case, since precisely, Mr Moser could not follow his profession in Germany, his only avenue was to go to another State where such restrictions did not exist.

In sharp contrast, of course, a U.S. citizen may have constitutional rights against her or his state government, even if the issue involves solely an internal matter within the state. The privileges and immunities and due process clauses of the Fourteenth Amendment have often been the basis of such claims.

[D]   The Effect of Article 14

CRIMINAL PROCEEDINGS AGAINST FLORUS ARIEL WIJSENBEEK
Case C-378/97, 1999 ECJ CELEX LEXIS 333, [1999] ECR I-6207

Note 1 The Court took no note of this fact in its reasoning. It was enough that the freedom being asserted was in connection with travel between Member States

Note 2 Q1 — The reasoning recognized that the law was in a state of developing — once harmonized rules could be applied at the external frontiers of the EC, it may no longer be necessary for Member States to check nationality.

Q2 — Although Wijsenbeek arrived at an airport where there were no incoming flights from outside the EU, the lack of harmonized external rules meant that the Netherlands could not be sure that he had not originally started his travel from outside the EU. This then justified maintaining the nationality checks.

Note 3 The judge was probably correct on that specific ground. Flynn would have had an Article 14 argument like Wijsenbeek, which, again, at the time, would have failed. With the adoption of such measures it is open to question whether article 14 might now have direct effect. This seems unlikely: *Echirolles Distribution SA v. Association du Dauphine* Case C-9/99 2000 ECJ CELEX LEXIS 645, [2000] ECR I-8207 where the Court declined to allow article 14 to be invoked against the French law on retail price maintenance for books (the law that had been the issue in the *Leclerc* case, Chapter 6, *supra*.)

[E]   The Effect of Article 18

BAUMBAST v. SECRETARY OF STATE FOR THE HOME DEPARTMENT
Case C-413/99, 2002 ECJ CELEX LEXIS 3461, [2002] ECR I-7091

Note 1 It is clear from this ruling that Article 18 has created a certain degree of freedom not previously incorporated in the EC Treaty, since it creates a right in principle to reside anywhere in the EU, at least as long as this does not create a financial burden for the host state.

Note 2 No, as Directive 2004/38 makes clear, even a person who does not rely in any way on the economic rights of free movement (for example a person who with ample means and private healthcare chooses to move to another Member State) remains subject in principle to the exceptions. However, the longer the residence, the more conditions are placed on the host Member State in seeking to expel an EU citizen.

KUNQIAN CATHERINE ZHU AND MAN LAVETTE CHEN v. SECRETARY OF STATE FOR THE HOME DEPARTMENT
Case C-200/02, 2004 ECJ CELEX LEXIS 493, [2004] ECR I-9925

Note 1 No economic activity permitting permanent residence was possible (given the age of the infant). Thus the only Treaty right was the general one under Article 18.

Note 2 The answer is clearly yes, it would have become a wholly internal matter. The result seems anomalous and probably not of more general application, because of the unique circumstances under which a person can be born in one Member State, of which she does not become a national by right of birth in that territory (*ius soli*) but does acquire the nationality of another Member State by reason of such birth.

Note 3 Mrs. Chen's right is derivative of her child's and might be considered equally based on the fundamental right of respect for family life (see Chapter 19).

GERALD DE CUYPER v. OFFICE NATIONAL DE L'EMPLOI
Case C-406/04, 2006 ECJ CELEX LEXIS 372, [2006] ECR I-6947

Note 1 Q1 — No. The case is the mirror image of most of the issues that arise in the area of social benefits. Here, Mr De Cuyper was unable to receive unemployment benefit from his own state because he was not resident there. This was therefore in no sense discrimination on grounds of nationality (see the following section of this chapter) with regard to entitlement to such benefits — and article 18 does not hinge on such a factor. Rather, the Belgian legislation had somewhat similar effects as that seen in cases such as Muller Faure (Chapter 10, supra). However, unlike that case, Mr De Cuyper could not claim rights under article 49 because his residence outside Belgium was not temporary in nature. Nor could he claim under article 43 since to assert establishment rights when claiming unemployment benefit would in and of itself have been enough to deny him the benefit. Thus his only argument was that his rights under article 18 were infringed. Article 18 would require an effect on interstate movement of some kind since wholly internal issues are outside the scope of existing EC Treaty provisions, but he was not debarred from asserting rights against his own Government any more than Mrs Muller Faure was under article 49.

Q2 — No, since his rights derived from article 18 and prior to its enactment, there would have been no other ground under which to claim. This of course was a peculiarity of his situation . . . had he been claiming some other benefit he might have been able to invoke article 43, subject however again to the kind of objective justification evaluation as the ECJ undertook here.

§ 18.03   NON-DISCRIMINATION

[A]   Derivative Rights

MICHEL S. v. FONDS NATIONAL DE RECLASSEMENT
SOCIAL DES HANDICAPÉS
Case 76/72 [1973] ECR 457

FRASCOGNA v. CAISSE DES DEPOTS ET CONSIGNATIONS
Case 157/84, [1985] ECR 1739

Note 1 Recalling the principles learned in Chapters 2 and 3, since regulations are directly applicable there is no latitude for Member States in terms of implementation, as there would be with directives. Moreover, they are invocable by individuals without the need to show direct effect, and are binding on everyone.

Note 2 Social security legislation has always had to reflect to a certain extent a certain moral choice, since these choices have to be made as part of defining entitlements. EU legislation in this regard is no different, and it may be argued that the ECJ should not be substituting its own moral views. On the other hand, since fundamental rights are an integral part of EU law, would not the legislation have to conform to such rights?

The second question in this note emphasizes that, despite the adoption of regulations in this area, there will still be significant divergences in the rights for individuals from one state to another.

[B]   Non-Discrimination in "Wholly Internal" Situations

ROMAN ANGONESE v. CASSA DI RISPARMIO DI BOLZANO SPA
C-281/98, 2000 ECJ CELEX LEXIS 321, [2000] ECR I-4139

Notes 1 and 2 The requirement in this case was by no means *intended* to discriminate against persons with foreign diplomas. It was meant only to ensure that employees in the Bolzano province of Italy were bilingual in Italian and German. Thus even other Italians were disqualified. This may seem a wholly internal situation perhaps not unlike *Moser*, or *Keck*, but the ECJ was not concerned by that, because it looked at the rule requiring the specific type of certification and determined that it would act against non-nationals. It remains to be seen whether the Court will eventually be drawn into a *Keck* type decision to avoid a charge that it is meddling in the internal affairs of Member States.

[C]   Indirect Discrimination

CRIMINAL PROCEEDINGS v. CHOQUET
Case 16/78, [1978] ECR 2293

Notes 1 and 2 (All questions) — *Choquet* is a good illustration of how Article 39 may apply to indirect discrimination. One might have expected that a Member State should be entitled to administer driving tests in its own language, and the Court does not explicitly require that states accommodate linguistic differences — only that all the aspects of such tests should be structured and administered in such a way as not to create excessive burdens on non-nationals, particularly where such nationals had already qualified in another Member State. While Article 39 is directed solely at nationality discrimination, rules of this kind would, when adjusted to reflect Treaty obligations, no doubt benefit a state's own nationals who had a foreign license, since the rules were not based on a distinction between nationals and non-nationals in the first place. *Choquet* is merely illustrative and the principles could apply in other areas, though this is perhaps limited because of the scope of Article 39.

Note 3 Had the *Choquet* case come before the courts in the United States, it is clear that the result, if not the reasoning, would be the same. Most if not all states in the United States require that, after a certain period of residency in the state, a person obtain a driver's license from that state, even if the person has a valid driving license from another state. Although such laws have apparently never been challenged in the courts on constitutional grounds, if they were, the courts would almost surely find that they constituted no burden on the right to travel and were a valid exercise of the state's police power. A state could not, of course, deny a person from another state with that state's driving license the right to drive as a transient in the state. But once such a person became a resident of the state and thereby "localized" the state would have the authority to demand that he obtain a local driver's license.

[D]   The Effect of Articles 12 and 18

FRANCOISE GRAVIER v. CITY OF LIEGE
Case 293/83[1985] ECR 593

Note 1 Vocational training is not built into the economic freedoms as such, but, Article 12, invoked in conjunction with other provisions of the Treaty conforming its application to vocational training was considered to create invocable rights. Note that no consideration was given to the "receipt of services" doctrine by the Court.

DAVID CHARLES HAYES AND JEANNETTE KAREN HAYES v. KRONENBERGER GMBH

Case C-323/95, 1997 ECJ CELEX LEXIS 292, [1997] ECR I-1711

Note 1 (All questions) — The connection with inter-state trade was to a large extent incidental. The rule in question clearly affected parties engaged in commercial transactions, and this could affect economic activity, thus it was sufficient to invoke Article 12. In the hypothetical, as in *Choquet*, (below) there seems no reason why the Court would not have reached the same conclusion since it was by no means necessary that the particular parties should have actually been engaging in commercial activity.

CRIMINAL PROCEEDINGS AGAINST HORST OTTO BICKEL AND ULRICH FRANZ

Case C-274/96, 1998 ECJ CELEX LEXIS 316, [1998] ECR I-7637

Note 1 The Court alludes to the parties as recipients of services and alludes to article 18 but generally discusses only the scope of Article 12. It does not therefore give any clear guidance as to whether the scope of the application of the Treaty referred to in Article 12 includes a standalone right under article 18.

Note 3 (All questions) — Apparently not, since the use of German was in the first instance determined as the basis of an examination designed to ascertain whether this was a mother tongue or not. The individuals were only entitled to the same treatment as Italian nationals in this regard. The ECJ is focused on equality but is not insisting on special rights to compensate for language difficulties where no law to that effect exists. Presumably this would be very much a question of criminal justice and thus may surface in EU law under the PJCC when that is moved to the EC Treaty.

MARIA MARTINEZ SALA v. FREISTAAT BAYERN

Case C-85/96, 1998 ECJ CELEX LEXIS 13186, [1998] ECR I-2691

Note 1 The case ventures into this territory by effectively creating a sort of estoppel. Once the state had, for any reason, allowed an EU national to take up residence, that state can no longer discriminate in the granting of social benefits by requiring the possession of a residence permit, since it does not require this of its own nationals.

THE QUEEN (ON THE APPLICATION OF DANY BIDAR) v. LONDON BOROUGH OF EALING AND SECRETARY OF STATE FOR EDUCATION AND SKILLS

Case C-209/03, 2005 ECJ CELEX LEXIS 98, [2005] ECR I-2119

Note 1 (Both questions) — The Court began by discussing the right of a Member State to deny financial assistance to non-nationals. This in principle still applies but not where the student is a lawful resident. In order to be a lawful resident, it is sufficient that he or she has been accorded that status by the host state and thus is not specifically dependent on the exercise of economic rights. The Court then examines the 3-year residence requirement to determine, on a *Cassis* type evaluation, whether it was justified (its being accepted that the rule applied equally to U.K. and foreign nationals). The requirement it appears could be justified on the basis of a need to demonstrate social integration. In this case, the Court avoided opening the floodgates to foreign students seeking financial assistance.

Note 2 It is still quite a narrow ruling, given the particular facts.

§ 18.04   EXCEPTIONS

[A]   Public Service Employment

COMMISSION v. BELGIUM
Case 149/79, [1980] ECR 3881

Note 1 In fact the Court had an extremely difficult time dealing with the Commission's complaint in this case. It recognized that the exception could be invoked for persons serving the state in an economic activity but had difficulty in setting clear guidelines as how to determine whether employees were exercising official authority. The exception would not usually apply to persons employed by a private company engaging a state granted monopoly because they would not be considered in public service.

Note 3 The advent of "European citizenship" casts into greater doubt the justification for excluding EU citizens from public service positions, because they seem in the vast majority of cases to be employment policies rather than having any connection with official authority. Moreover, as often already noted, the Members States' authorities often act as the EU's "agent" in the implementation and enforcement of EU policies.

[B]   Public Policy

VAN DUYN v. HOME OFFICE
Case 41/74 [1974] ECR 1337

Note 2 (Both questions) — The Court considered that the exception would be deprived of its value if it could not be used in circumstances such as Mrs Van Duyn's even though the UK. The very purpose of the exception was to enable a Member State to refuse admittance to a non-national while of course nationals would always be entitled to enter the country even if they were engaged in known undesirable activities.

ALFREDO ALBORE
Case C-423/98, 2000 ECJ CELEX LEXIS 383, [2000] ECR I-5965

Note 1 This case interestingly arose under article 56. The State requirement might have some justification in the frontier zones bordering non-EU countries but is unlikely to find support in the Court for frontiers adjoining other Member States since it would be hard to find any convincing rationale.

[C]   Activities Outside the Scope of the EC Treaty

UNION ROYALE BELGE DES SOCIETES DE FOOTBALL ASSOCIATION ASBL AND OTHERS v. JEAN-MARC BOSMAN
Case C-415/93, 1995 ECJ CELEX LEXIS 220, [1995] ECR I-4921

Note 1 It is perhaps at first sight surprising that the Court was prepared to entertain any argument that discrimination on grounds of nationality is justifiable. However, the only possibility of success for such an argument would be based on the need for only nationals of a Member State to represent that state in international matches, which would be considered outside the scope of application of the EC Treaty, presumably due to its non-economic characteristics (though this is a bit of a stretch given the financial implications of such matches for many organizations including broadcasters). This surely had nothing to do with the arrangements at issue in *Bosman* as the Court indeed concluded.

§ 18.05   VOTING RIGHTS

MATTHEWS v. UNITED KINGDOM
(App. no. 24833/94) EUROPEAN COURT OF HUMAN RIGHTS (1998) 28 EHRR 361, [1999] ECHR 24833/94

Note 1 The EU Treaty now contains a reference to the ECHR and the ECJ and CFI increasingly refer to it. However, this does not make the ECHR a part of EU Law. Thus this case dealt only with the U.K.'s position under the ECHR. It does illustrate the potential for a collision at some point, as Member States seek to implement EU Law.

M. G. EMAN AND O. B. SEVINGER v. COLLEGE VAN BURGEMEESTER EN WETHOUDERS VAN DEN HAAG
Case C-300/04, 2006 ECJ CELEX LEXIS 446, [2006] ECR I-8055

Note 1 The case does not in fact hinge in any way on the rights of citizenship as such but on a breach of the EU rules relating to elections to the European Parliament and specifically the principle of equal treatment for all nationals of a Member State. That said, these are clearly aspects of citizenship, and the rules in question might be considered a precursor of their status.

Note 2 Since the action in dispute here was that of a Member State, redress would have to be against the Member State. The real question is why at this stage of its evolution, the EU does not have an EU wide electoral law that determines all aspects of elections to the Parliament. That said, it should be recalled that elections in the U.S. also are largely governed by State laws, although disputes ultimately can be brought to the Supreme Court through the certiorari process: *Bush v. Gore* 531 U.S. 98 (2000). In providing redress through the courts, an EU Member State could be held accountable for breach of EU fundamental rights, much as the U.S. Supreme Court may assess a state to have violated the Fourteenth Amendment.

Chapter 19
PERSONAL RIGHTS

§ 19.02   HUMAN DIGNITY

OMEGA SPIELHALLEN — UND AUTOMATENAUFSTELLUNGS — GMBH v. OBERBURGERMEISTERIN DER BUNDESSTADT BONN
Case C-36/02, 2004 ECJ CELEX LEXIS 458, [2004] ECR I-9609

Note 1 The ECJ invoked the ECHR here to *justify* state action on grounds of public policy based on an affront to human dignity. One may imagine therefore that the Charter, with its identical provisions, would in future be invoked to the same end. In the US, the complainants might well have asserted First Amendment rights, and there seems in principle to be a similar argument open under the Charter, yet this was not mentioned. Thus, what has happened here is that the *State* invoked the charter against what might have been a corresponding *individual* right had it been asserted. The ECHR then, and by derivation, the Charter, seem to be a catalogue of values rather than rights where state/social/economic interests are pitted against individual freedoms as well as other specific economic freedoms guaranteed by the Treaties. We seem to be many years away from seeing how this balancing act might start to coalesce into some general principles, inevitably driven by the political and social background of the judges — which finds echoes in the US Supreme Court.

§ 19.03   FREEDOM OF EXPRESSION

LASERDISKEN APS v. KULTURMINISTERIET
Case C-479/04, 2006 ECJ CELEX LEXIS 447, [2006] ECR I-8089

Note 1 (All questions) — The freedom of expression issue in this case raises the questions regarding the right to receive information and ideas. The plaintiff had sought to argue that the directive's approach, which allowed a copyright owner to prevent dissemination of a work in the EU when it had previously been put into circulation outside the EU (no "international exhaustion" — see the *Tesco/David off* case set out in chapter 8), entailed a restriction on the rights of EU residents to receive the information and ideas of the copyrighted work. The argument was really without merit because the directive didn't actually prevent access to non-EU works. As the Advocate-General described it:

> "The claimant submits that the principle of Community exhaustion is contrary to the freedom of expression enshrined in Article 10 of the European Convention on Human Rights, since its effect is to prohibit imports from third countries and thus prevent citizens from receiving information.

> That article states that everyone is to have the right to freedom of expression, which includes freedom to receive and impart information and ideas without interference by public authority and regardless of frontiers. It is common ground that Article 10 covers the expression of ideas by means of film.

> The European Union is required to respect fundamental rights as guaranteed by the Convention.

> Prohibiting international exhaustion does not of course equate to prohibiting imports from third countries. It does however mean that certain items protected by copyright and related rights and not distributed within the Community may not be available in the Community or may be so available only at a price higher than the lowest price which obtains outside the Community.

> Since the author of such an item can ensure that it is available throughout the

Community by putting it on the market in any Member State, it is clear that the principle of Community exhaustion does not infringe the author's freedom to impart ideas.

On the other hand, prohibiting international exhaustion might in principle affect the right to receive ideas, since a person within the Community wishing to acquire such an item may find that he cannot, or can do so only at a price higher than that charged outside the Community. However, the Court of Human Rights has stated that the right to freedom to receive information basically prohibits a Government from restricting a person from receiving information that others wish or may be willing to impart to him'. Prohibiting international exhaustion involves no restriction on the right as so expressed.

Even if the Court were to conclude in the present case that there was a restriction on the freedom of expression, that restriction would in my view be justified. Article 10(2) of the Convention provides that the exercise of freedom of expression, since it carries with it duties and responsibilities, may be subject to such formalities, conditions, restrictions or penalties as are prescribed by law and are necessary in a democratic society . . . for the protection of the . . . rights of others'.

The Court has held that the exercise of the right to freedom of expression may be restricted, provided that the restrictions in fact correspond to objectives of general interest and do not, taking account of their aim, constitute disproportionate and unacceptable interference, impairing the very substance of the rights guaranteed. The interests involved must be weighed having regard to all the circumstances of the case in order to determine whether a fair balance was struck.

It seems clear that the choice of mandatory Community exhaustion rather than optional international exhaustion reflects a satisfactory balancing of the interests involved. The regulation of intellectual property rights in the Community inevitably reflects an attempt to balance the competing interests of the rightholder and the free movement of goods. The Copyright Directive explicitly seeks to achieve this balance: the preamble stresses both the importance of the internal market and the need for a high level of protection of intellectual property. Recital 3 moreover emphasises that the legislature was aware of the conflicting interests, stating that the proposed harmonisation relates to compliance with the fundamental principles of law and especially of property, including intellectual property, and freedom of expression and the public interest'.

The Court has stated that, in terms of Article 10(2) of the Convention, specific restrictions on the exercise of the right of freedom of expression can, in principle, be justified by the legitimate aim of protecting the rights of others'.

It has also stated that the discretion enjoyed by the national authorities in determining the balance to be struck between freedom of expression and the objectives mentioned in Article 10(2) varies for each of the goals justifying restrictions on that freedom and depends on the nature of the activities in question. When the exercise of the freedom does not contribute to a discussion of public interest and, in addition, arises in a context in which the Member States have a certain amount of discretion, review is limited to an examination of the reasonableness and proportionality of the interference. That holds true for the commercial use of freedom of expression.

It seems to me that there is nothing in the present case to suggest that the choice by the Community legislator of mandatory Community exhaustion rather than optional international exhaustion was either unreasonable or disproportionate."

BERNARD CONNOLLY v. COMMISSION
Case C-274/99 P, 2001 ECJ CELEX LEXIS 687, [2001] ECR I-1611

Note 1 The AG describes essentially a four step process of analysis:

1. Does the law or action in question actually interfere with the freedom of expression?
2. Does it serve one of the enumerated legitimate purposes?
3. Is it sufficiently precise that individuals can know whether they are obeying the law or not?
4. Even if all of the above are satisfied, is the restriction necessary in a democratic society?

In *Connolly*, there could not be much doubt as to where the Court would land, based on this type of approach. While there was obviously an overt restriction on the freedom of expression arising from the requirement for prior permission and the possibility of refusal, a refusal in this case would have been legitimate based on the need to preserve trust between the institution and an official charged with carrying out its official policy. Even then, it was not so much the criticism of policy itself but the attacks on Commission employees that was the concern here. The rule itself allowed the required predictability because it simply required Connolly to obtain prior permission which he failed to do. And there was certainly nothing to suggest the restriction was unusual in a democratic society, given the need for the public to be able to place reliance on civil servants' carrying out the tasks for which they have been appointed.

Having said that, one can only conclude that every case is going to be fact specific, since the steps in the analysis provide for a lot of flexibility. Overall however one may conclude that there will be a bias in favor of legality of restrictions, since the EU is certainly under extreme constraints as regards any possibility of enacting laws or taking decisions that would constitute flagrant violations of fundamental rights.

VEREINIGTE FAMILIAPRESS ZEITUNGSVERLAGS — UND VERTRIEBS GMBH v. HEINRICH BAUER VERLAG
Case C-368/95, 1997 ECJ CELEX LEXIS 316, [1997] ECR I-3689

Note 1 In the first instance, the question was whether the Austrian law that prohibited giveaways by newspapers infringed article 28 EC. This involved a *Cassis* evaluation because the rule wasn't specifically aimed at imports. In carrying out the evaluation, the national court would need to assess whether the objective justification might itself fall foul of the fundamental EU right to freedom of expression since a free press is an essential element of the principle (parallels with the *ERT* case here). This then entailed a further step in the evaluation based on the ECHR principles as to legitimacy of the limitation. That evaluation would depend on whether the Austrian policy aimed at protecting smaller newspapers that could not compete with more well funded larger papers was disproportionate to the aims of that policy. Ultimately that question was left for the Austrian courts to determine with not a lot of guidance from the ECJ.

§ 19.04   THE RIGHT TO OWN PROPERTY

HUBERT WACHAUF v. THE STATE (BUNDESAMT FÜR ERNÄHRUNG UND FORSTWIRTSCHAFT) (FEDERAL OFFICE FOR FOOD AND FORESTRY)
Case 5/88, 1989 ECJ CELEX LEXIS 435, [1989] ECR 2609

REGINA v. MINISTRY OF AGRICULTURE, FISHERIES AND FOOD EX PARTE BOSTOCK
Case 2/92, 1994 ECJ CELEX LEXIS 95, [1994] ECR I-955

Note 1 (All questions) — In Bostock the court explicitly rejected the notion that the right to dispose of an EU entitlement, such as a reference quantity, could be considered as a property right. In that case the tenant had surrendered his lease, so the property right if there were one would have to have been an independent standalone right, which was what the court expressly rejected.

By contrast, in Wachauf the tenancy had expired and the lessor refused to renew it. Mr Wachauf had been a dairy farmer and all the equipment belonged to him. He would have suffered financial loss if there were no compensation due to the transfer of the reference quantity to his lessor. However, while the Court recognized that the EU regime provided for compensation in such circumstances, there was no assertion as such that such an entitlement could be considered a property right. This surely must have been the case in some sense, otherwise why would compensation be due at all?

These two cases therefore leave one in considerable confusion as what "property" might mean in the ECHR and the Charter.

§ 19.05   EQUALITY

DIRECTIVE 75/117
1975 O.J. L45/19

DIRECTIVE 76/207
OJ 1976 L 39/40

M. HELEN MARSHALL v. SOUTHAMPTON AND SOUTH-WEST HAMPSHIRE AREA HEALTH AUTHORITY
Case C-271/91, 1993 ECJ CELEX LEXIS 174, [1993] ECR I-4367

Note 1 Ms Marshall was able to invoke article 6 of the directive because her employer was a government run facility. She was thus able to invoke the directive directly to have the cap on damages removed. This is essentially then an assertion of her EU rights regarding gender discrimination. A claim on the other hand against a private employer would have had to be followed by a claim against the government for compensation for failure properly to implement the directive.

Note 2 The Court objected fundamentally to the notion that a cap on damages could be appropriate given the variety of situations and the level of loss suffered by an individual. To remove the cap for cases involving claims for compensation against the government based on the directive while maintaining the cap for claims against private employers would only create further litigation against the government for failing properly to implement the directive, so the ultimate result was that the cap on damages for discrimination cases was abandoned altogether. This could be well be considered to defeat other arguably legitimate reasons for imposing such a cap, such as predictability for employers. The possibility of legitimacy for caps based on a legitimate social purpose however seem to have been inferentially completely rejected by the Court.

Note 3 (Both questions) — The "not less favorable" criterion is only a baseline. It would be sufficient where EU law did not require a higher standard, but that was not the case here. This is generally reflective of the ECJ's willingness to insist on remedies where a directive addresses the rights of individuals, presumably as a specific expression of the will of the EU in such cases.

J. P. JENKINS v. KINGSGATE (CLOTHING PRODUCTIONS) LTD
Case 96/80, [1981] ECR 911

Note 1 The Court set a fairly tough standard for plaintiffs to meet — that "the pay policy. . . . cannot be explained by factors other than discrimination based on sex". Thus if the employer can offer some rational objective reason for the policy, the disproportionate impact on the disadvantaged sex would not be enough to violate article 141.

Note 3 If as other cases suggest, the burden is on the employer to prove that there is an objective justification, this might be considered an unfair tilting of the balance in favor of employees, and it could be argued that this violates the principle of equality.

BARBER v. GUARDIAN ROYAL EXCHANGE ASSURANCE GROUP
Case 262/88, 1990 ECJ CELEX LEXIS 147, [1990] I ECR 1889

Note 1 Clearly the future effects of this decision had the potential to be significant because of the cost implications of bringing the treatment of men in line with that of women, this assuming that the apparently more favorable treatment of women would be the baseline. It would be possible however to move in the other direction, but this could raise arguments that would reflect badly on EU law and also be contrary to an alleged fundamental principle that the incorporation of fundamental rights into the legal fabric of EU law should not have the effect of reducing existing rights. This was a factor in the *Mangold* case as well: underlying the Court's judgment may have been a concern that, absent the overriding principle of equality, the later directive could be construed as condoning more age discrimination than had previously been permitted under national law.

Note 2 (All questions) — The *Barber* case highlights a real contradiction as between, on the one hand, the adoption of fundamental rights applicable to the scope of EU law, and on the other, persistent discrimination by Member States with regard to matters firmly in their area of control. The operation of social security schemes containing discriminatory treatment for men and women is one such area. The Court is well aware that any ruling that condemns such schemes would likely result in a backlash from the Member States. It is unlikely therefore that the directive would be considered invalid. Yet, it is not impossible to make the point that social security, which affects so profoundly EU rights such as those in article 43 and 141 ought to be considered within the scope of EU law. (See in this regard the introduction of language into the EC Treaty by the Treaty of Lisbon.) This sort of argument was what in all likelihood lay behind the UK government's concerns regarding the enactment of the Charter and its effects on labor relations in the UK. Although the Charter states that its scope of application extends only to matters within the scope of EU law, it becomes increasingly difficult, given the amount of social legislation at the EU level, to argue that nonetheless the Charter has no effect on matters such as the right to strike (or rather, limitations on that right).

KATARINA ABRAHAMSSON AND LEIF ANDERSON v. ELISABET FOGELQVIST
Case C-407/98, 2000 ECJ CELEX LEXIS 377, [2000] ECR I-5539

Note 1 The Court rejects the principle of affirmative action to the extent that it involves allocation of jobs based on gender regardless of merit. It condones only criteria that are intended to remove disadvantages suffered by women — as for example a seniority requirement based on full time service, which would adversely affect women who had resorted to part time working to bring up children. This approach might be analogized the US Supreme Court's 2007 decision in *Parents Involved in Community Schools v. Seattle School District No. 1* No 05-908 (June 28, 2007), 551 U.S. ___ (2007) regarding allocation of school places based on race. Justice Kennedy indicated that detailed alternative plans, such as drawing attendance zones that recognize neighborhood demographics, recruiting students and faculty in a targeted fashion and tracking enrollments and performance by race, could be acceptable. Such methods, Justice Kennedy wrote, are "race-conscious, but don't lead to differential treatment based on race classifications".

GABRIELE HABERMANN-BELTERMANN v. ARBEITERWOHLFAHRT, BEZIRKSVERBAND NDB./OPF. E.V.
Case C-421/92, 1994 ECJ CELEX LEXIS 173, [1994] ECR I-1657

Note 1 (All questions) — As in the *Mangold* case, the German law in issue here was actually meant to provide support for those in the plaintiff's situation, not discriminate against them. In the narrow sense, the case itself concerned only the question of whether the contract could be treated as void due to the common mistake of the parties in believing that Mrs. HB was able to work night shifts. Obviously, her pregnancy did not prevent this permanently. The ECJ did not call into question the validity of the German law, which was expressly endorsed by Directive 76/207, but rather the application of a Civil Code provision that would have allowed the contract to be treated as void, in which event Mrs. HB would have lost her job altogether. It is hard to imagine however that the employer would not have been justified in declining to employ her on account of her condition if he had known of it, because he and she would both have been aware that from the date of employment and for as long as the legal prohibition on night work applied to her, she would not actually have been permitted to perform the duties that she had expressly requested. To rule against the employer because he had mistakenly hired her establishes a point of principle but on rather difficult facts.

§ 19.06   RESPECT FOR FAMILY LIFE AND PRIVACY

LISA JACQUELINE GRANT v. SOUTH-WEST TRAINS LTD
Case C-249/96, 1998 ECJ CELEX LEXIS 308, [1998] ECR I-621

Note 1 *Grant* involved the application of social security laws where the Member States retain control. Thus, the case did not concern the application of EU law by a Member State and thus EU fundamental rights were not applicable, including of course the right to a "family". One may speculate therefore as to what the Court might do when confronted with questions where it is necessary to define that term.

MARY CARPENTER v. SECRETARY OF STATE FOR THE HOME DEPARTMENT
Case C-60/00, 2002 ECJ CELEX LEXIS 261, [2002] ECR I-6279

Note 1 The case would seem to have the consequence that any non EU national married to a national who is exercising EU rights is subject to a different régime with regard to immigration status than someone who is married to a national who is not exercising such rights. It is truly difficult to understand why such a difference in treatment should exist; perhaps it is time to abandon it and treat citizenship as an absolute right, not connected to the exercise of economic rights.